songwriting secrets

BRUCE SPRINGSTEEN

Learn from the greats and write better songs

BRUCE SPRINGSTEEN

Learn from the greats and write better songs

Rikky Rooksby

Author of *How to Write Songs on Guitar*

songwriting **secrets**

Bruce Springsteen

Rikky Rooksby

A BACKBEAT BOOK
First edition 2005
Published by Backbeat Books
600 Harrison Street
San Francisco, CA 94107, US
www.backbeatbooks.com

An imprint of The Music Player Network, United Entertainment Media Inc.

Published for Backbeat Books by Outline Press Ltd,
2A Union Court, 20-22 Union Road, London SW4 6JP, England
www.backbeatuk.com

ISBN 0-879308-36-2

To Kevin Groves, and Alan & Steve Bennett

*"In order to understand the song's intent, you needed to invest a certain
amount of time and effort to absorb both the music and the words. But that's
not the way a lot of people use pop music."*
BRUCE SPRINGSTEEN, *Songs* (1998)

EDITOR John Morrish
DESIGN Paul Cooper Design

Origination and Print by Colorprint (Hong Kong)

05 06 07 08 09 5 4 3 2 1

contents

preface

Songwriting Secrets is a new kind of artist-focused music book.

This book does not tell you how to play specific songs by Bruce Springsteen. There are no transcriptions of Bruce Springsteen's music within these pages. If you want to learn his songs seek out sheet music from the appropriate publishers; for the lyrics consult his excellent illustrated book *Bruce Springsteen Songs* (Virgin/Avon, 2003). *Songwriting Secrets* is for songwriters and listeners who want to understand some of the rock and folk formulas Springsteen has used in his songs.

This book takes the thoughtful reader deeper into the music, x-raying its structures and revealing some of its codes. By looking at Springsteen's songs in this way you can have a better understanding both of his music and of the common currency of techniques which make it up. This currency belongs to everyone who has ever written a song, or wanted to write a song. Grasping what Springsteen has done with these traditional ideas reveals something about his music-making and simultaneously suggests possibilities which others – including you – could develop in your creativity.

Songwriting Secrets is a book of opportunity and possibility. Chords, progressions, structures for choruses, 12-bars, ideas for lyrics, band arrangements are just a few of the subjects laid out. In addition, the book includes a career overview and an annotated discography for Springsteen's 30-year recording history. Within these pages are many tips and ideas that can find new life in your own songwriting, even if the style and themes of the music you play are a long way from those of this American giant. And after exploring these pages you'll hear Springsteen's music in a new way.

Rikky Rooksby

introduction

*"Because the record company, Rosie,
Just gave me a big advance ..."*
'ROSALITA (COME OUT TONIGHT)'

So sang a 24-year-old man from Freehold, New Jersey, in 1973. For 30 years Bruce Springsteen has written songs, made records and thrilled audiences with impassioned concerts. He has released more than 200 songs, written many hits for other artists, and, despite letting about 80 previously unreleased numbers out on the *Tracks* 4 CD box-set and the bonus third disc of *The Essential Bruce Springsteen*, undoubtedly has many more in the archive. He is a rock legend who has forged an abiding connection through his music with the lives of millions. There is much that aspiring songwriters can learn from him.

Springsteen has spoken in broad terms about the themes of his music. He published a short commentary on his lyrics in the book *Bruce Springsteen Songs*, and occasionally he's discussed the way certain of his albums were made. But he has not said much about the nuts- and-bolts of songwriting – of how he thinks about purely musical issues such as song structure, chord patterns, melody notes, etc. True, he almost never gets asked about it. Perhaps, like many creative people, he is wary of looking too deeply in that direction lest he muddy his inspiration with too much self-consciousness.

That's where this book comes in. *Songwriting Secrets Bruce Springsteen* is a handbook of techniques observed at work in the music of one of the most successful songwriters of the past 30 years. This handbook provides insights into the common currency of songwriting and what Springsteen did with these patterns in his own songs.

These tips, tricks and patterns are not exclusively his, nor did he invent them. Nor would he necessarily think about his music from this angle. Most songwriters are intuitive, trusting their ear as to what sounds right. This book traces, after the event, the fingerprints left on a body of work. These ideas rise from the common musical language used by songwriters. Each person takes these ideas and impresses their own personality on them and expresses their own concerns through them. Musical ideas are amazingly flexible. Lock 100 songwriters in a room with a guitar and the instruction to compose a song with the chords D, G and Bm, and you will get 100 different songs. If Springsteen is among the 100 he might produce 'If I Should Fall Behind'. Think of it this way: everybody's handwriting is different, yet everyone writes with the same alphabet.

Songwriting secrets … but of which Springsteen?

So, does this book show how to write a Bruce Springsteen-type song. Yes … but which type of Springsteen song would you like to write? He has written songs in a variety of styles. There's a long, hard road from the joyful funk of 'The E Street Shuffle' to the eerie ballad 'Empty Sky'.

For many, Springsteen is the acme of American 'blue-collar' rock, a guy who sings about cars, girls and not much else. This is probably how he was seen by much of the global audience he momentarily reached with the *Born In The USA* album: a pumping, sweaty, unsubtle stadium rocker, a sort of Rambo of the six-string. If this were a true picture he would not be an artist of stature. Uneven as his work sometimes is, there is a core of greatness to his best music that puts him in the exalted company of the very best and gives his music a dignity rock does not often attain. This core transcends the totting up of chart positions and platinum discs.

In fact, Springsteen has made some starkly contrasted music. The Woody Guthrie-ish folk tales of *The Ghost Of Tom Joad* could not be further from the raw rock of *Darkness On The Edge Of Town*; the synth-pop of 'Dancing In The Dark' is a long way from the gritty but adventurous funk of 'Kitty's Back'; and the modern production of *The Rising* is nothing like the Spectoresque wall-of-sound of *Born To Run*. From celebrating the mythic romance of the American Dream he has gone to exposing its limitations, and the plight of those who crawl at its margins and under its shadow. Having seen his ambivalent feelings about the US in 'Born In The USA' distorted and co-opted (by Ronald Reagan and others) into a simplistic, ungrounded patriotism, he responded to the events of 9/11 in a way that was artistically successful and avoided hate-fuelled jingoism.

In Springsteen's career, commercial and critical acclaim have not always coincided. The populism of his *Born In The USA* period alienated many, even if they knew who he was before. In the 1990s critical acclaim came with albums like *The Ghost Of Tom Joad*, in which he positions himself deliberately in a tradition of American folk songwriting, and his one-man-and-a-four-track album *Nebraska* has been favourably re-assessed. This re-positioning is reflected in the more mumbled timbre of his recent singing, in contrast to the soulful funkster of the second album and the chesty Presley/Orbison vocals of *Born To Run* and *Darkness On The Edge Of Town*.

Of course, no one can formularise the deeper energy that makes Springsteen write in the first place and compose in the way he does. That energy is part of him, channelled through the boundaries of his musical knowledge, craft, desires, and other aspects of the music business that affect the options an artist considers when making records for so large an audience. This is true of all composers: the inaccessible songwriting secret is what makes them them. It's a matter of fundamental identity. When Springsteen sits down to write a song he brings to it every experience he's had since he was born.

However, there is a whole layer of craft and songwriting knowledge through which that identity is expressed. And that's what this book sets out to illuminate. This book is not a critical appraisal of Springsteen's music. It doesn't discuss his lyrics at length or his socio-musical context. It is a hands-on guide to his composing in the context of popular songwriting. So how did Springsteen emerge and what musical context did his talent grow in?

The road from Freehold

Born in 1949, Bruce Springsteen grew up in Freehold, New Jersey. Asbury Park was a nearby seaside town, 53 miles from New York. Elvis on the Ed Sullivan Show in 1958 inspired him to ask for a guitar when he was nine, which he got. But, like many youngsters who try to learn, he found it hard and put it aside. The musical urge waited for another chance. At 13 he bought his second guitar from a pawnshop and joined local band The Castiles in 1965. With them he played his first professional gig in nearby Woodhaven. They made a demo in 1966 with two songs co-written by Springsteen. Springsteen absorbed the British Invasion bands – The Stones, The Animals, The Who – and then Motown and Atlantic soul.

This variety of influence has stood him in good stead; he has never forgotten the magical immediacy of mid-1960s pop and rock. Chris Humphries described him in concert as "a one man history of rock'n'roll, a human jukebox". Dave Marsh called Springsteen "the living culmination of 20 years of rock & roll tradition". In 1980 Springsteen commented, "I've been influenced by a lot of people. Elvis was one of the first. Otis Redding, Sam Cooke, Wilson Pickett, The Beatles, Fats Domino, Benny Goodman, a lot of jazz guys. You can hear them all in there if you want to."

Moving with musical fashion, by the late 1960s Springsteen had long hair and played heavy blues-rock on a Les Paul in bands like Earth, Child, Clearwater Swim Club and Steel Mill (formed in 1969). In 1999 Springsteen called Steel Mill "riff-oriented hard rock". The Mill gigged in California (on the first of two ventures into the West that Springsteen seems to have made), and were offered a recording contract, but returned to Asbury Park. This band included E-Streeters Vini Lopez and Danny Frederici. It split in 1970. Then followed short-lived line-ups like Dr Zoom and the Sonic Boom and The Bruce Springsteen Band. All the while Springsteen gained vital experience as a live performer. According to 'Miami' Steve Van Zandt, "He was into songwriting very early on and was always quite good at it. There weren't that many people writing back then; it was still the era of the old Brill Building thing. Recalling what happened after the trip to California, Springsteen said, "I moved from hard rock to rhythm-and-blues-influenced music and I began to write differently." By 1971 he knew it was time for a change.

Springsteen got going with his own material partly by default. "The main reason I started doing my own arrangements and writing my own songs was because I hated to pick them up off the records. I didn't have the patience to sit down and listen to them, figure out the notes and stuff." (1978) He then ran into one of the difficulties of trying to play his music. "Nobody would book us (in the early 1970s) because we never did any Top 40. Never. We used to play all old soul stuff, Chuck Berry, just the things we liked. That's why we couldn't get booked. We made enough to eat, though." (1982)

Into the studio

When Springsteen signed a management contract with Mike Appel in 1972 he had no band. He played solo for noted A&R man John Hammond at CBS in May 1972. Hammond saw Springsteen as a new Dylan folk-singer type. But when recording for the first album started in June 1972, Bruce insisted on a band. By this point Springsteen had seven years songwriting behind him in several styles. The lyrics were wordy – and would eventually get cut back – and the impressionistic songs had a cinematic quality, with an imagined landscape and characters. Some were long: Springsteen was experimenting with longer forms that would work well live. He had plenty of experience of trying to win over audiences. This was an important facet of his songwriting influences. He later described *Greetings From Asbury Park, N.J.* as "an acoustic record with a rhythm section". He was confident enough as a songwriter to write 'Blinded By The Light' and 'Spirit In The Night' because Clive Davis, the head of the record label, said there were no singles on the LP.

There is a whole audience that didn't pick up on Springsteen until *The River* and another crowd that got on board for *Born In The USA* and quickly drifted away. If only they had heard the albums Springsteen made before the breakthrough with *Born To Run* (1975). Both have the unselfconsciousness quality that early recordings tend to possess and which, once lost, cannot be recovered.

In 1973 many critics dismissed Springsteen as a mix of Dylan and Van Morrison. His own personality and musical strengths were obscured. The first version of the E Street Band toured with Chicago to promote *Greetings*. For the second album, *The Wild, The Innocent and the E Street Shuffle*, they explored a funkier, direct music with electric guitars, and worked on the longer dramatic songs. Springsteen wanted to inject a dose of bar-band sparkle'n'clatter into the new songs to up the energy of the band's live show. 'Rosalita' quickly established itself as one of the highlights of the stage-set. The 1978 film clip of this song did much to promote the image of Springsteen abroad.

The second album appeared in February 1974. The numbers lengthened, as did the sets. In May 1974, journalist and later Springsteen producer Jon Landau wrote the famous review which featured the quote: "I saw rock'n'roll's future and its name is Bruce Springsteen." His profile grew, and with the band almost out of money and almost dropped, he started the third album, the one that had to be a killer. Roy Bittan replaced David Sancious on piano and Max Weinberg came in on drums.

Reverse into self

Released in August 1975, *Born To Run* saw Springsteen simplify his musical vision. His first two albums had sold moderately, and Springsteen was building a reputation as a live act. But it was *Born To Run* that lit the fuse to stardom. Not for nothing did Springsteen name-check Roy Orbison singing for the lonely in 'Thunder Road'. Reaching past hard rock, Springsteen's landmarks were late 1950s / early 1960s: Orbison, Presley, The Righteous Brothers, The

Ronettes, The Beach Boys, Bo Diddley, Duane Eddy, Phil Spector. Critic Greil Marcus once described 'Born To Run' as a "'57 Chevy running on melted-down Crystals records". Roy Bittan said of it: "He said he wanted a record where the singing sounded like Roy Orbison." Springsteen himself said in 1987, "I wanted to make a record that would sound like Phil Spector. I wanted to write words like Dylan. I wanted my guitar to sound like Duane Eddy." The album "spoke the traditional language of rock'n'roll". In October 1975 both *Time* and *Newsweek* put him on their covers – he was "Rock's New Sensation".

Unable to record thereafter, due to a legal dispute with manager Mike Appel, Springsteen toured more. The sets edged up to 26 songs and sometimes lasted over four hours. His fourth album, *Darkness On The Edge Of Town*, was finally released in June 1978. There were no grand epics, the arrangements and production were sparser than previously, and the subject matter was darker. Excepting 'Candy's Room', there is little that is musically adventurous, though the songs have a raw power. Springsteen said he wanted the album to be relentless. It was followed in 1980 by *The River*, a 20-song collection that again showed simplicity in the songwriting. It culminated in the audacious but possibly ill-advised attempt to stretch three chords and two bars of music to nine minutes on 'Drive All Night'. Springsteen said of it, "On *The River* I would tend to have songs that were kind of celebrations and darker songs next to each other. That was because I didn't know how to synthesise it into one song. I knew it was all part of the same picture, which is why *The River* was a double album."

Going back to roots

No one could have guessed Springsteen's next album *Nebraska* (1982) would be a set of demos recorded on cassette. Searching for inspiration and cultural roots, Springsteen read a biography of Woody Guthrie. It inspired him to cover Guthrie's 'This Land Is Your Land' in concert, which Guthrie had written as a reply to Irving Berlin's 'God Bless America'. Springsteen also listened to early Johnny Cash and Hank Williams. 'Born In The USA' emerged from Springsteen's engagement with a pre-rock'n'roll tradition of folk songwriting and protest. In 1987 Springsteen recalled, "*Nebraska* was rock bottom. I came home from tour and I sat down for two months and I wrote the whole thing. I recorded and mixed it in my bedroom and put it out on cassette. I always think of it as my most personal record. What happens when all the things you believe in when you're 25 don't work? What happens when all these things just break down? Your friends fail you, or you fail your friends? When you're alone – can you live? Can you go on?"

His next move took him back to rock and to the commercial highpoint of his career: *Born In The USA* (1984) sold more than 10 million copies in the US alone and ushered in the era of the biceps, the headband, the denim jacket, the stadia. The title track was inescapable. Festival crowds sang it with gusto when it boomed out through PAs, whether they were American or not. "I had written a catchy song and I felt it was a really good song, probably one of my best since 'Born To Run'. I knew it was going to catch people – but I didn't know it was going to catch them like *that*, or that it was going to be what it was." On June 1st 1985 in Ireland he played to 70,000 people, his biggest audience so far.

Reflecting on the success of *Born In The USA*, Springsteen said, "I wouldn't *mind* having another big record like that. But my main concern is writing the new song that has that new idea, that new perspective. To me, that is the essence of my job ... Also, you want to rock people. That's my job too. So that makes you want to write a *fast* song."

After that, it was time to rein back and scale down. Working independently of The E Street Band, Springsteen attempted with *Tunnel of Love* (1987) to cut an intimate record to resist the forces that might make him too distant from his audience. It was his first record to focus on love relationships in a domestic context. He said, "I wanted to write a different kind of romantic song, one that took in the different types of emotional experiences of any relationship where you are really engaging with that other person and not involved in a narcissistic romantic fantasy or intoxication or whatever."

The conservative songwriter

Though there is much to admire in Springsteen's music there are some areas that act more as warnings to a songwriter looking to learn from him. He has had much critical praise for his lyrics, understandably because those lyrics express positive, humane qualities and sentiments. Sometimes the music on which these lyrics are hung is not as interesting as it could be. Springsteen deliberately simplified his music when he fell in love with the roots 'authenticity' of the folk tradition represented by Cash, Guthrie, and Williams. This has sometimes been a detrimental influence. Music can redeem lyric clichés but it doesn't work the other way round.

His prolific songwriting rate suggests an artist who is not primarily concerned with creating new musical progressions and structures. His focus is on the words and the imagined world the lyric evokes. He is content to re-use standard forms and sequences, as we shall see. This can lead to him writing by formula in the 1980s and 1990s. Most songwriters have blind spots – things they unconsciously repeat. He has the arrangement cliché of the dynamically quiet last verse, and the middle-eight that starts with chord IV of the key he is in.

A further point is that, like Dylan, Springsteen is not a great melodist. His best songs are sometimes great in spite of their melodies rather than because of them. They suffer from being too linear, with too many repetitions of the same note sung in succession, and move in a narrow pitch range. So, in 'No Surrender' the melody remains on the 5th note of the scale (C in F major) for six bars in the verse. In 'I'm Goin' Down' it sticks around the key note Bb too much. Listen to 'Cautious Man' and 'Walk Like A Man' one after the other – the latter's opening melody sounds close to the previous song. The tune of 'Better Days' in parts is close to the melody of a phrase from 'The River'; "Is a dream a lie if it don't come true?" To hear a Springsteen song such as 'The Angel', or 'Counting On A Miracle', with a more angular melody and a wider compass, is a pleasant shock. For example, the little-known 'Sad Eyes' is splendid melodically, with Springsteen singing falsetto to get the high notes.

Through the 1990s Springsteen wrote and recorded *Human Touch* and *Lucky Town* (1992), and returned to a folk style for *The Ghost Of Tom Joad*. His songwriting took a new turn on *The Rising* (2002), where he was reunited with The E Street Band and updated their rock sound for the new century. In recent years sell-out tours indicate he has lost none of his appeal for his audience.

How to use this book

Songwriting Secrets: Bruce Springsteen is a resource. It has many well-tried chord sequences that belong to everyone. It will fill gaps in your knowledge and suggest new techniques to shape your material and adapt to your style. If you have a half-complete song that's missing a section, look through these pages and find an idea. If you seem always to write the same kind of song with a similar progression or structure it will give you ways out. If stuck for inspiration, dip into *Songwriting Secrets: Bruce Springsteen* at random.

Each technique is illustrated with citations of Springsteen songs, though there are no transcriptions of his actual music. The idea is that you go and listen to the song referred to, check out the technique as it happens in that song, and then go and use it yourself. The book assumes you have many of these albums or can get hold of them. There may be more than one citation for a given song, so check the index if you have favourites. The fact that such different-sounding songs may use the same technique proves the flexibility of many of these ideas.

The book has five sections. Section 1 looks at common structures for songs which Springsteen has used. This includes information about intros, verses, choruses, middle-eights, and the 'long form' songs that were once a Springsteen hallmark and vital to the success of his live shows.

Extended songs don't work without a feeling for how an audience responds to a song's twists and turns. Section 2 looks at the chord sequences that fill these structures. It covers the two-chord song, the I-VI change, the three-chord trick, displacing and withholding chords, the role of inversions, four, five and six-chord songs, and so on.

Section 3 looks at the business of making music in the studio and on stage, with observations about instrumentation and arrangement. Section 4 focuses on the guitar in Springsteen's music, and Section 5 tackles lyric-writing. There is a discography of Springsteen albums, an appendix explaining a few basic bits of theory useful to songwriters, and an index of song titles.

To find out more on chord sequences, melody, lyrics, guitar chords and guitar tunings, have a look at *How To Write Songs On Guitar* (2000), *The Songwriting Sourcebook* (2003), *Chord Master* (2004), and *Melody* (2004). If you write riff-based songs, *Riffs* (2002) is the most encyclopaedic study ever published about them. To learn more about songwriting, arrangements and the elements that make a magic recording, try *Inside Classic Rock Tracks* (2001), where 100 songs from 1960 to the present day go under the microscope. Information about these titles can be found at http://www.Backbeatbooks.com and http://www.rikkyrookysby.com.

verses and choruses

How do songwriters shape their ideas into manageable chunks? How do they shape the raw material of musical inspiration into a form that other people can enjoy and find memorable? How do you start a song? How do you end it? How long does it have to be? This section gives ideas for the individual parts of songs: intros, verses, choruses, bridges and endings.

INTROS
'CANDY'S ROOM', 'THUNDER ROAD'

Intros matter, though songwriters often neglect to give them enough thought. The first few seconds of a song are important – so don't just stick with the first thing that comes to you. The intro is where you can grab a listener's attention, state a theme, set an atmosphere, get a concert hall jumping. You can tell Springsteen understands this because of the gusto with which he counts off many of the songs, "1 ... 2 ... 3 ... 4 ... !" He even made such a count a feature of 'Born To Run', where it introduces the last verse.

A survey of Springsteen's songs throws up a number of possible intros. You could try the simple approach: four bars on the key chord, as in 'Better Days'. 'Rendezvous' comes in on a drum-beat and Bruce's interrupted count before hitting the sus2 /sus4 riff – which is essentially still a one-chord intro. Both 'Streets Of Philadelphia' and the 2001 live version of 'Atlantic City' enter with only a drum-beat, in the latter leaving the audience to guess the song. The brooding atmosphere of 'Stolen Car', with its muted strumming and distant piano, is fixed from the outset by its quiet intro on one bass note and two chords. By contrast, 'Born In The USA' takes no prisoners with its keyboard hook and cracking snare drum. This intro is sheer muscle but reserves any continuous beat and chording for verse 2.

How about starting, as many Springsteen songs do, with loud, accented chords separated by pauses? Think of 'The Ties That Bind' or 'Prove It All Night'. Such intros suggest the power of a rock band without using it all by extended playing. You can recycle an intro later in the song. 'Prove It All Night' brings back its intro after the second chorus just before the sax solo. That's a very effective way of allowing band and audience to catch their breath in the middle of a song and gets more mileage from the musical idea of the intro itself. The sax solo in 'Prove It All Night' hits harder because of it. 'Night', from *Born To Run*, is another powerful start to a song with a frenetic machine-gun guitar chord of Csus2 with the snare-drum struck in the same rhythm. Some of Springsteen's intros are extended into instrumental passages. 'Seaside Bar Song' uses one minute of its 3:33 duration on an instrumental beginning. 'Backstreets' takes a good 1:08 to reach the first vocal and verse. 'Something In The Night' goes for a quiet build-up intro on chords I and IV.

The 'false' intro

A 'false' intro is not in some way wrong. It's an intro that intentionally misleads the listener to enhance the impact of what follows. It makes listeners think they know what sort of a song it will be, only to find it turn out quite different. A false intro can start in one musical style but reveal its true one only on reaching the verse.

'Tenth Avenue Freeze-Out' starts with four bars of gently descending brass chords which are not yet the nagging two-chord change of its main intro. 'The E Street Shuffle' has a comic intro that playfully suggests the brass section warming up. It takes 12 seconds to settle into the basic groove of the song. 'Lonesome Day' is a mild example of a 'false' intro. It starts on an F chord that might be taken as the key chord, except that the key is actually Bb and the F is chord V.

Your false intro can start at a different tempo, time or key to the first verse, as in this example where the intro is in A major but the verse in F major. Try strumming the chords to hear the effect:

False intro

Verse

I		VI		II		V		I		VI		V		IVm[VI]	
A	/	F#m	/	Bm	/	E	/	A	/	F#m	/	E	/	Dm	/

I			
F	/	/	/

(The chord names are on the lower line. The music is assumed to be in 4/4, four beats to a bar. Roman numerals above the chords describe their harmonic function in the home key, here A major in the first four bars, followed by F major in bar five. This is a useful shorthand for describing chord relationships which all songwriters should learn. If it is new to you have a look at the appendix, where it is explained.)

One of Springsteen's finest beginnings to a song is 'Candy's Room'. This is a good example of a false intro starting with a spoken vocal. Spoken vocal intros can be kitsch and melodramatic, but here the combination of Springsteen's low mumble, the spattering hi-hat and the sparkle of the keyboards and glockenspiel works brilliantly. The delayed entry of the full band at the word "kiss" extends the intro. Only on the word "wild', with its firm C major chording, does it feel as though the song is fully underway.

The recycled intro

A 'recycled' intro forms part or all of a later section such as the bridge or chorus. It has the advantage that when the first chorus proper is reached the listener has already heard the sequence and it is half-familiar. This gives your first chorus a sense of returning to something instead of being a new thing.

'Waiting On A Sunny Day' keeps the same sequence through intro, verse and chorus. 'My

Love Will Not Let You Down' uses the same sequence for its intro as the verse and the chorus (the prechorus is different). If you wish to contrast the intro's later appearance with its first, you can use the same chord sequence in different keys. On the other hand, try writing a song where the intro's progression is the only one of the entire song. 'Point Blank' has an intro which supplies the chord progression that drives the entire song.

The free time intro

A 'free time' intro is one without an obvious beat, which creates suspense. Play your chords to support each vocal or instrumental phrase by arpeggiating on the piano or guitar, one note at a time (no continuous strumming). Let the chord ring while a few vocal phrases are sung with small pauses between them. This emphasises the meaning of the words, if there are words.

'Thunder Road' begins with just harmonica and piano, no drums, no felt pulse. After a few phrases the piano and harmonica lock into a slowly accelerating tempo which leads to the first sung words; the drums do not enter until later. 'New York City Serenade' opens with David Sancious's free-time piano solo of a virtuoso kind that pays homage to George Gershwin and the spirit of his *Rhapsody in Blue*. Only after a while does the piano settle into a regular pulse once it starts playing the chord progression of the verse (see the discussion of this song under 'Long form song' below).

THE 8-BAR FORM
'NO SURRENDER', 'I'M GOIN' DOWN'

Songs tend to have three main sections: a verse, a chorus, and a bridge (or middle-eight). In addition, they often have an intro and a coda (an epilogue, a final bit after the last chorus), sometimes a solo, and sometimes a 'prechorus' – an extension to the verse that leads to the chorus and which you can repeat later in the song independently of the verse.

The most popular lengths of section tend to be multiples of four. Songs often have 4-, 8-, 12- and 16- bar sections, with or without a repeat. There is something about the symmetry of a 4-bar phrase, especially with four beats in a bar and possibly four chords, which has a strong appeal. Multiples of four shape the structure of most of Springsteen's songs. If you're relatively new to songwriting, try these lengths.

'No Surrender' has an 8-bar verse and an 8-bar chorus, both of which start on chord I. The instrumental 'Paradise By The 'C'' opens with an 8-bar section. 'I'm Goin' Down' has a single 8-bar sequence for verse, chorus and sax solo. 'Cadillac Ranch' and 'Born In The USA' have single 8-bar sections which serve for verse and chorus. 'Cover Me' and 'Youngstown' have a traditional middle-eight – a bridge made up of eight bars. 'Straight Time' has an 8-bar verse and an 8-bar chorus, although only the first four bars of the chorus are sung over. 'The New Timer' and 'You Can Look (But You Better Not Touch)' have 8-bar verses. 'Hungry Heart' has an 8-bar verse made up of a 4-bar phrase repeated.

You can make an 8-bar section in several ways. It could be the result of a 4-bar phrase repeated:

4-bar idea in G

I				IV				V				IV			
G	/	/	/	C	/	/	/	D	/	/	/	C	/	/	/ :‖

Or it might not have a repeat, but be eight different bars. Here are two examples of an 8-bar structure suitable for a verse, chorus or bridge. The key is G major and the chords are limited to three: chords I, IV and V, which in a major key are always major.

8-bar idea in G

I				I				IV				I			
G	/	/	/	G	/	/	/	C	/	/	/	G	/	/	/

IV				V				I				I			
C	/	/	/	D	/	/	/	G	/	/	/	G	/	/	/

Another 8-bar idea in G

I				IV				V				IV			
G	/	/	/	C	/	/	/	D	/	/	/	C	/	/	/

I				IV				V				V			
G	/	/	/	C	/	/	/	D	/	/	/	D	/	/	/

THE 12-BAR FORM
'DARLINGTON COUNTY', 'I'M ON FIRE', 'COVER ME'

Your next option is to structure your song around 12-bar forms. There is an important distinction to be made when considering the 12-bar structure. Chords arranged in any pattern can make a 12-bar section; it can result from repeating a 4-bar phrase three times; or you might make it by adding an 8-bar phrase to a 4-bar phrase. However, the label '12-bar' often implies a set form for three particular chords.

With this specific meaning, the '12-bar' is one of the most frequently-used structures in the history of popular music. It shapes a huge percentage of blues songs. From blues it passed to 1950s rock'n'roll and is present in many songs by Chuck Berry, Elvis Presley, Little Richard, Jerry Lee Lewis, etc. It passed to 1960s pop and soul, regaining its blues roots during the

British blues boom and the heavy, psychedelic rock that was influenced by the blues revival (Hendrix, Cream, Free, Led Zeppelin). It featured in 1970s glam-rock, and is still used today.

If you want to try it, here is an example of a traditional 12-bar. Note that chord I fills bars 1-4.

12-bar in G

I				I				I				I			
G	/	/	/	G	/	/	/	G	/	/	/	G	/	/	/

IV				IV				I				I			
C	/	/	/	C	/	/	/	G	/	/	/	G	/	/	/

V				V				I				I			
D	/	/	/	D	/	/	/	G	/	/	/	G	/	/	/

In Springsteen's music this traditional 12-bar is used in songs like 'Cross My Heart' (in E) and 'Open All Night', a straight 12-bar in F. '57 Channels (And Nothing On)' has a 12-bar variant in which chord I lasts eight bars, the remaining four being conventional.

Another interesting variation you can try is to take out chord I from the last four bars so they look something like this:

Alternate end, bars 9-12 in G

V				V				IV				IV			
D	/	/	/	D	/	/	/	C	/	/	/	C	/	/	/

The verse of 'Tenth Avenue Freeze-Out' has a 12-bar format in which there is no return to chord I in the last few bars – that chord is saved for the chorus. Its 12-bar runs four bars of a I-VI change, two bars of a IV-II change, two bars of I-VI again, finishing with two bars of V and two of IV.

The 12-bar form is very flexible. It can feature in any part of a song – a verse, chorus or bridge – and you do not have to be writing an actual blues song. It is now such a familiar structure that listeners recognise it and know where it is going. You can use the 12-bar to effectively contrast with sections that are less formulaic and perhaps more demanding to listen to. Notice how the *rate* of chord change (how often chords change) is slow – chord I occupies the first *four* bars. Chord V is delayed until bar nine.

If you need more ideas, this next 12-bar includes two popular alternatives. There is now a change to chord IV in bar two. This gives such a 12-bar the name 'quick-change'. The second feature is that in bars 9-12 there is now more chord activity.

Quick-change 12-bar

I				IV				I				I			
G	/	/	/	C	/	/	/	G	/	/	/	G	/	/	/

IV				IV				I				I			
C	/	/	/	C	/	/	/	G	/	/	/	G	/	/	/

V				IV				I				V			
D	/	/	/	C	/	/	/	G	/	/	/	D	/	/	/

In the next variation the chords in bars 9 and 10 are reversed from the traditional order:

12-bar in G (variation)

I				IV				I				I			
G	/	/	/	C	/	/	/	G	/	/	/	G	/	/	/

IV				IV				I				I			
C	/	/	/	C	/	/	/	G	/	/	/	G	/	/	/

IV				V				I				I			
C	/	/	/	D	/	/	/	G	/	/	/	G	/	/	/

You can feel free to mess about with these structures to make them fit your lyric or progression. A 12-bar can keep its basic structure but elongate by a few bars. The listener hears it as a 12-bar with a repeated phrase on the end, or an extension:

12-bar variation to 14 bar verse

I				I				I				I			
G	/	/	/	G	/	/	/	G	/	/	/	G	/	/	/

IV				IV				I				I			
C	/	/	/	C	/	/	/	G	/	/	/	G	/	/	/

V				IV				V				IV			
D	/	/	/	C	/	/	/	D	/	/	/	C	/	/	/

I				I		V		
G	/	/	/	G	/	D	/

Sometimes the 12-bar is extended by doubling the number of bars to a chord (making a 24-bar). 'Pink Cadillac' is an elongated 12-bar in which the 20-bar verse has eight bars of I, four of IV, four of I, and four of V. It should have four bars of E to make 24 but they're omitted; the chorus is a straight 12-bar. 'Ramrod' (in F#) shows an elongated 12-bar. 'The E Street Shuffle' doubles the bars and adds two extra chords to it (VI and bVI). 'Darlington County' is a stretched 12-bar that also doubles the number of bars. 'She's The One' combines Bo Diddley rhythm, sus4 chords and a 12-bar in E with the number of bars doubled.

If you combine a 12-bar verse with an 8-bar chorus you create a blueprint for a complete song.

Remember that a 12-bar structure does not have to be restricted to the blues format and those three chords. 'None But The Brave' has a 12-bar section with the chords I, IV, V, and VI. This is an example of a four-chord 'non-blues' 12-bar.

THE 16-BAR FORM
'DANCING IN THE DARK', 'WORKING ON THE HIGHWAY'

If you have written songs with 8- and 12-bar sections, the next level to progress to is the 16-bar. Along with the 12-bar, 16 bars is the most popular length for a verse section. A 16-bar section can be handled in many ways, depending on the amount of repetition. Your symmetrical options for structuring the 16 bars are:

*   a 2-bar phrase played 8 times;
*   a 4-bar phrase played 4 times;
*   a 4-bar phrase played 3 times with a different phrase for bars 9-12;
*   a 4-bar phrase played 3 times with a different phrase for bars 13-16;
*   an 8-bar phrase followed by a four bar phrase repeated, or *vice versa;*
*   an 8-bar phrase played twice;
*   a single 16 bar phrase, with no repeats.

Quite a lot of choice! Of these, the second is probably the most common in popular songwriting, followed by the next two options. The last option is the rarest because it requires more planning. Here are some templates you can adapt:

16-bar verse in G

I				I				ii IV				I			
G	/	/	/	G	/	/	/	C/G	/	/	/	G	/	/	/

I				I				V				IV			
G	/	/	/	G	/	/	/	D	/	/	/	C	/	/	/

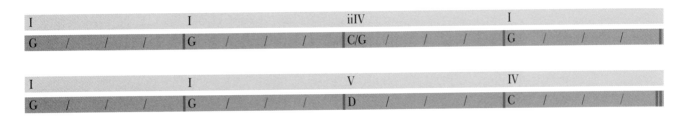

As the list of permutations above shows, most 16-bar sections are not actually made up of 16 different bars. Some lines have their chords repeated, as here:

16-bar verse in G (variation)

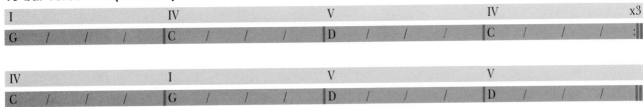

Though 16 bars long, the above verse is a 4-bar phrase played three times with a final 4-bar phrase to comment on the one that's been heard three times. This would make a typical 16-bar structure.

In Springsteen's output, 'Dancing In The Dark' has a 16-bar verse in which a 2-bar phrase is repeated four times before there's a change, an 8-bar chorus and an 8-bar middle-eight. 'Highway 29' has a 16-bar verse. 'Jackson Cage' has a 16-bar verse, the first 4-bar phrase repeated, the second half featuring a rising bass-line. 'Two Hearts' has a 16-bar verse made up of an 8-bar section, using chords I and IV, which is repeated. 'The River' has a 16-bar verse made of a single section. 'Atlantic City' has a 16-bar verse made up of a 4-bar phrase repeated four times with a change of final chord on the fourth time.

Explore the 16-bar structure. You will find many, many ways to fill it with chords, divide it into bits, and wrap your words around it.

THE 'MULTIVERSE'
'INCIDENT ON 57TH STREET'

So far we've looked at song sections constructed on the numbers 4, 8, 12 and 16. You may be curious to know: is it possible to go further? And if so, how? The answer is postpone the chorus, build the anticipation. You do this with a new concept in verse-writing: the 'multiverse'. 'Multiverse' is a term I coined to describe a more complex verse form than is normal in rock songs. It's a verse which has more than one section, causing a delay of the chorus.

Many songwriters never write multiverses, but there are a number in Springsteen's earlier music. 'Thunder Road' is one example, as is 'Incident on 57th Street'. 'Incident' is a love song lasting 7:44 with subtle dynamics and the cinematic quality typical of Springsteen's second album. It has the extended song structure Springsteen often deployed at this time, which schematically looks like this (timings and lyric cues are given for the start of each section):

Intro

Verse 1:

Section A = 'Spanish Johnny' 0:28

Section B = 'pimps' 1:08

Section C = 'Puerto Rican Jane' 1:38

Chorus 1 = 'Good-night' 2:15

Verse 2:

Section A = 'cruel' 2:49

[Section B missed out]

Section C = 'Puerto Rican Jane' 3:24

[Chorus 2 omitted]

Verse 3:

Section A = 'sitting' 4:00

Section E = 'romantic' 4:43

Choruses repeat to fade

Coda: solo piano

It can be seen from this breakdown that 'Incident' has a three-part first verse, a chorus, an edited second verse, and then just when we expect chorus 2 the music is stripped back to a vocal and a bass guitar for a variant of the verse at 4:00. The last chorus is only finally reached after a delightful (organ) suspended chord at 5:02.

You can learn an important lesson about repeated choruses at the end of a number from this song. It ends with four choruses, each one of which builds in intensity. Chorus 2 is sung gently, and at 5:18 beautiful backing vocals appear. Chorus 3 picks up a bit in intensity, and in chorus 4 distorted electric fills out the middle of the picture. On this chorus Springsteen really tugs at the melody and ends with a sustained note which is picked up in chorus 5 by a guitar solo. The faders are pulled back on most of the instruments except the ethereal backing vocals and the piano. The E Street Band roars into the distance, followed by the voices, leaving only the chiming piano arpeggios to segue straight into a guitar-driven live favourite, 'Rosalita (Come Out Tonight)'.

Live In Barcelona features a solo piano version of this song.

Here's a tip for writing a 'multiverse'. If you've written a song and want to extend it, take your chorus and add it onto the verse, then write a new chorus. Then adjust the original chorus so that it isn't going to overshadow the new chorus. This might mean thinning out some of the chords, having fewer changes, restricting the choice of chords, etc. Some people find it easier to arrive at a multiverse this way than to sit down and try to think of a verse with several bits to it.

Another multiverse technique is if you limit yourself to the three major chords of a major key for your verse, saving the minor chords for later, try writing a section that starts on each of those three major chords. That will give you a three-section multiverse. If you think these chords are not interesting enough, give them a new slant by using their inversions. So a multiverse in the key of G major would have chords G, C and D as the main chords, and their inversions would be G/B, G/D, C/E, C/G, D/F#, and D/A. For more information about inversions see the section on Bruce's chords.

BRIDGES AND MIDDLE-EIGHTS
'THE RISING', 'MARY'S PLACE', 'BRILLIANT DISGUISE'

Once you have a verse and a chorus written you may want to consider having a third bit. Songs often have a third section – a bridge or middle-eight – to contrast with the verse and the chorus. It's not essential (and might be unnecessary in a song with a multiverse) but usually, after two verses and two choruses, we feel the need for the music to go somewhere new. This makes a later return to a verse or chorus fresher. The bridge can offer a chance for your lyric to introduce new images and ideas. You could also put a solo at this point, before or after the bridge, or instead of a vocal bridge.

There is a simple song form that comprises a verse alternating with a bridge. There is no chorus; the 'hook' is included at the end of the verse. The Beatles used this approach during their early years of success. In Springsteen's catalogue 'Two Faces' would be an example of this form.

One easy way for your bridge to break new musical ground is to introduce a new chord or chords. These would have been withheld from use earlier in the song. Try writing the verse and chorus with only chords I, IV and V, and save a minor chord or chords for the bridge.

There are plenty of examples to follow in Springsteen. 'The Rising' (in Bb) is a three-chord song where a fourth, Gm (chord VI in Bb) is saved for the guitar solo. 'The Fuse' has D, Am, C and G for its verse and chorus; its middle-eight brings in a long stretch of Bm (chord III in G). In 'Mary's Place' the sax break centres around a Dm (chord VI in F) previously not heard in the song. 'Working On The Highway' saves Am (chord VI in C) for its middle-eight. 'Be True' (A) starts its bridge on F# minor (chord VI of A). 'She's The One' has a middle-eight whose first six bars are entirely on the three minor chords in the key of E major (F# minor, G# minor and C# minor) before a B chord (chord V) leads the music back to a stretch of E major sax solo.

By contrast, 'Youngstown' is in G minor and starts its middle-eight on Eb (chord VI, a major chord). So, if the song is in a minor key you could do the reverse of what happens in a major key song. Bring in a previously-unheard *major* chord for the bridge if your verse and chorus have minor chords.

Bridges that start on IV

One Springsteen formula, which became an unconscious reflex in his songs of the 1980s and 1990s, is to start the middle-eight on chord IV, regardless of whether it has been used earlier or not. If you want to try this follow this example, where the link sets the harmonic scene coming out of a chorus.

Eight-bar bridge starting on IV

[link]

I				VI				I				VI			
D	/	/	/	Bm	/	/	/	D	/	/	/	Bm	/	/	/

[middle-eight]

IV				IV				IV				I			
G	/	/	/	G	/	/	/	G	/	/	/	D	/	/	/

IV				IV				I				V			
G	/	/	/	G	/	/	/	D	/	/	/	A	/	/	/

The following Springsteen songs all have bridges/middle-eights that start on chord IV of whatever key they happen to be in: 'Across The Border', 'Streets of Philadelphia', 'From Small Things', 'All That Heaven Will Allow', 'Spare Parts', 'Cautious Man', 'Gloria's Eyes', 'Real World', 'Man's Job', 'I Wish I Were Blind', 'Local Hero', 'If I Should Fall Behind', 'Leap Of Faith', 'The Big Muddy', 'Souls of the Departed', 'My Beautiful Reward', 'I Wanna Be With You'. 'Cover Me' (a minor key example), 'Johnny 99', 'Highway Patroller', 'Atlantic City', 'Two Hearts', 'I Wanna Marry You', 'Happy', 'Brothers Under The Bridge ('83)', 'I'm On Fire', 'Better Days', and 'Blood Brothers'.

I would estimate that possibly up to quarter of all the songs Springsteen has released start their bridges on chord IV. This indicates how important it is for songwriters to develop as much objectivity about their songwriting habits as they can.

There are dangers in unconsciously repeating yourself. Of course, everyone has a blind spot. But when six songs on the same album (*Lucky Town*) all do this there is a risk that listener will feel they sound too similar. For similar reasons, check the keys of your songs when you're constructing the running order of an album. Unless there are compelling reasons to do otherwise, never put more than two songs in sequence that are in the same key, and think carefully even when doing this.

Bridges that start on V

To give your bridge a bolder start try kicking it off with chord V of whichever key the song is in, instead of chord IV. Chord V has a slightly stronger, more bracing effect than chord IV. Here is an example in E major:

8-bar bridge starting on V

[link]

I				IV				I				IV			
E	/	/	/	A	/	/	/	E	/	/	/	A	/	/	/

[middle-eight]

V				V				VI				VI			
B	/	/	/	B	/	/	/	C#m	/	/	/	C#m	/	/	/

II				II				IV				IV			
F#m	/	/	/	F#m	/	/	/	A	/	/	/	A	/	/	/

Though he does so far less often than using chord IV, Springsteen has songs that commence a middle-eight on chord V. Examples include 'Brilliant Disguise' (in A, bridge starts on E); 'Living Proof', 'A Good Man Is Hard To Find' (in D, bridges start on A); 'My Lover Man', 'Something In The Night', 'Mary Lou' (in G, bridges start on D); and 'Ricky Wants A Man Of Her Own' (in E, bridge starts on B).

Another option for you to try is to have a bridge start on one of the three minor chords of the major key. Springsteen's 'Secret Garden' starts its bridge on chord VI (Am) in C major to good effect.

THE 'EIGHT PLUS ONE' TRICK
'BOBBY JEAN', 'WORKING ON THE HIGHWAY'

Or, the middle-eight that isn't eight! It's sometimes fun and effective to do something to change the predictability of sections that are simply multiples of four. There are two practical reasons why you might want to do this. First, the lyric may have a word or a phrase which makes it too long to fit into the eight bars, so you add a bar or more to provide musical room for the phrase to be sung. Second, the '8+1' trick lends itself to postponing the next section, be it a solo, a verse or a chorus, in order to generate a tense build-up of some kind.

There is an easy way to change the length of a bridge from the expected eight bars to another number. First, try a literal '8+1': add a bar onto an eight-bar section like a middle-eight:

'8+1' middle-eight in A major

IV				IV				VI				VI			
D	/	/	/	D	/	/	/	F#m	/	/	/	F#m	/	/	/

IV				III				I				V			
D	/	/	/	C#m	/	/	/	A	/	/	/	E	/	/	/

V			
E	/	/	/

You can hear this in 'Two Hearts', which has an '8+1' bridge with an extra bar of chord V as a build-up tacked on the end, and in 'Bobby Jean', which is also an '8+1' example.

But why stop there? So next, add two bars on, to give yourself a 10-bar section:

10-bar bridge in G

II				III				I				VI			
Am	/	/	/	Bm	/	/	/	G	/	/	/	Em	/	/	/

II				II				III				V			
Am	/	/	/	Am	/	/	/	Bm	/	/	/	D	/	/	/

VI				V			
Em	/	/	/	D7	/	/	/

(It would have been easy to repeat bars 1-4 as 5-8 but this is more interesting. Second time round, the change to Bm is delayed by a bar, creating the chance for suspense.)

Next, why not add three bars? This 11-bar bridge features a major version of chord II (which is usually minor in a major key) that suggests the music is about to change key from C major to G major. However, the next chord cancels out that expectation.

11-bar bridge in C

III				VI				III				VI			
Em	/	/	/	Am	/	/	/	Em	/	/	/	Am	/	/	/

VI				II ^				IV				bVII			
Am	/	/	/	D7	/	/	/	F	/	/	/	Bb	/	/	/

V				IV				V			
Gsus4	/	/	/	F	/	/	/	G	/	/	/

In Springsteen's songs, 'Working On The Highway' has an 11-bar bridge which consists of a two-bar VI-I change, followed by a bar of chord IV and then four bars of chord V as a build-up. 'The Fuse' has a 14-bar bridge using two chords D and Bm (I and VI). 'Hearts Of Stone' combines a 13-bar verse with an eight-bar chorus. Its last verse adds one more bar of chord V to make 14 bars to delay the entry of the last chorus. 'My Hometown' has a 16-bar (double-length) middle-eight which starts on chord VI withheld until then, and the first minor chord to appear in the song.

LONG FORM SONGS
'THUNDERCRACK', 'ROSALITA (COME OUT TONIGHT)', 'JUNGLELAND', 'NEW YORK CITY SERENADE', 'DRIVE ALL NIGHT', 'LAND OF HOPE AND DREAMS'

Most songs last between three and four minutes. They have two, three or four verses, possibly three or four choruses, and a bridge. Longer songs are usually the province of progressive rock bands and tend to have lengthy instrumental passages – think of The Doors' 'Light My Fire', where the bridge organ/guitar solo grows to epic proportions. Springsteen had his own intepretation of the extended song. Let's round off Section 1 of this book with a schematic plan of some of his 'long form' songs. From this you could take some ideas for setting some of your longer lyrics.

Long form songs offer opportunities for sax and guitar solos but also multiple climaxes, extempore sections, chances for talking, etc. They are good for lyrics that have a story to tell through many verses. In Springsteen's work they include the laid-back minor-key swing of 'The Fever'; the striking 'Frontline' (recorded 1972) which clocks in at 7:20 and has several bridges that wander away from the home key; 'Thundercrack', and songs that became highlights of Springsteen's live-set, notably 'Rosalita (Come Out Tonight)'. (At the other extreme, possibly the shortest Bruce song, is the frantic live cut 'Held Up Without A Gun', at a frantic now-you-hear-it, now-you-don't 1:09.)

The long form song was one way Springsteen saw of getting people's attention in concert. He knew the difficulties firsthand: "I had all this stuff stored up for years, because there was no outlet in the bars I had been playing. No one's listening in a bar, and if they are, you've got a low PA system and they can't hear the words anyway." In *Songs*, he explained, "In '74 I had to have songs that could capture audiences that had no idea who I was. As an opening act, I didn't have much time to make an impact. I wrote several wild, long pieces – 'Thundercrack', 'Kitty's Back', 'Rosalita' – that were arranged to leave the band and the audience gasping for breath. Just when you thought the song was over, you'd be surprised by another section, taking the music higher. It was, in spirit, what I'd taken from the finales of the great soul revues." Eventually Springsteen figured out how to deliver the same punch in a shorter form – in the song 'Born To Run'. But note his reference to soul revues. This is an influence that has given his rock music an element of drama that many other rock bands don't have. It's a drama explicitly concerned with connecting to the audience.

Learning and recording such long songs could be an arduous process for the musicians. Keyboard player Roy Bittan commented, "We were recording epics at the time. I mean, 'Jungleland' and 'Backstreets' are not easy songs to record. It's like trying to drive a Grand Prix course: every time you go around one turn, there's another." Roy Bittan also played with Dire Straits, whose third and fourth albums also have a number of long form songs derived entirely from the Springsteen model, rather than from other 1970s UK bands like Genesis and Yes who played long pieces.

■ 'Thundercrack' (9:32), key of G major

When Springsteen started performing concerts to support the first album he wanted to write material that had the physical impact of rock. He said, "The song 'Thundercrack' was something that we wrote as the showstopper. It ended three or four different times – you didn't know where it was gonna go. It was just a big, epic show-ender that was meant to leave the audience gasping a little bit for their breath." That it certainly does.

As you look over this plan, notice the numbers two, four and eight controlling the phrase and section lengths. This long song uses less music than you might think. Small sections are repeated and that's how the length is built up. Notice in the chords column which chords are heard in which section and the way some chords are held back until later on in the song. It is also important for a long song to vary the instruments heard at any time, so instruments enter for some sections and are omitted for others to give light and shade.

Section	Phrase	Repeats	Total	Chords	Notes
Intro	4 bars	x 2	8	I IV V	vcls, bv, gtr, tempo 88
	4 bars	x 2	9 (8+1)		
Intro 2	2 bars	x 4	8	I IV V	tempo 116
	2 bars	x 4	8		organ in
	2 bars	x 4	8		'sha-na-na' vcls
Verse 1	2 bars	x 4	8	(intro 2)	drums, lead vcl in
Chorus	4 bars	x 2	9 (8+1)	I IV V	
Verse 2	2 bars	x 4	8		
Chorus 2	4 bars	x 2	9 (8+1)		
Chorus 3	4 bars	x 2	8		'round and round' bvs
Bridge	4 bars		4	VI III II IV V	1st use of minors
Verse 3	2 bars	x 3	6		
	4 bars		4	VI I	extension
Sax solo	10 bars		10	VI IV II III	
Guitar link	8 bars		8	no chords	cres. /lead-in

Instrum. verse	2 bars	x 8	16	I IV V	guitar lead
	2 bars	x 8	16		guitar + sax
	2 bars	x 4	8		guitar descend.
	2 bars	x 4	8		guitar + sax
	2 bars	x 8	16		guitar + sax descend.
	2 bars	x 4	8		static note
Verse 4	2 bars	x 3	6		vocals back in
Chorus 4	4 bars	x 2	9 (8+1)		
Chorus 5	4 bars	x 2	8		'round and round' bvs
Bridge	4 bars		4		
Verse 5	2 bars	x 3	6		
Coda	2 bars	x 8	16	I IV V	'all night'
	2 bars	x 4	8		sax 'A'
	2 bars	x 4	8		as 'all night'
	2 bars	x 4	8		sax 'A'

◼ 'Rosalita (Come Out Tonight)' (7:00), key F major

'Rosalita' was the successor to 'Thundercrack'. In 1999 Springsteen said, "'Rosalita' began to fill that spot in the show and held it for many, many years, probably the best song I ever had for that particular function." It had also been anticipated by 'Seaside Bar Song', which was only 3:33 long but a more complex form than usual, with several musical and lyric phrases sounding like 'Rosalita'.

It's immediately apparent from the chords column that there is more going on in 'Rosalita' than in 'Thundercrack'; there's less reliance on chords I, IV and V, and the inclusion of several more adventurous sections as far as harmony goes. (The ^ sign next to a Roman numeral means that the chord might normally be expected to be a minor or a diminished but it has been turned into a major chord.) Listen in particular for bridge 2 (4:19-56) where the tempo uses a half-time feel – it sounds slower but the actual beat is still the same. The original beat returns with the unaccompanied vocal on "papa says he knows". Half-time is a clever way of changing the rhythmic feel of a song without the complications of altering the time signature or the tempo to something which is more awkward.

Section	Phrase	Repeats	Total	Chords	Notes
Intro	2 bars	x 4	8	I	partial band
	2 bars	x 4	8		full band
Verse1	2 bars	x 8	16	I IV V	vocal in
Prech.	12 bars		12	IV III VI V	4 bar V cres.
Verse2	2 bars	x 4 only	8		
Prech.2	12 bars		12	IV III VI V	4 bar V cres.

continued on next page

Chorus	2 bars	x 4	8	I IV V	
Link 1	2 bars	x 4	8	[as chorus]	sax solo
Verse3	2 bars	x 8	16	I IV V	
[Extension]	4 bars	-	4	IV V	
Prech.3					
Chorus2	2 bars	x 4	8	I IV V	[no sax solo]
Bridge1	8 bars		8	V-bVII all ^	chromatic/ instr.
	8 bars		8	VII ^	build-up
Solo	2 bars	x 8	16	I IV V	sax + guitar
Link2	4 bars	x 2	8	I II bIV	tonic pedal
Bridge2	8 bars	x 2	16	V II VI III	vocal, half-time feel
	6 bars		6	IV V I III VI	
	6 bars		6	[V implied]	*a capella* vocals, b/v
Prech. 4	8 bars		8	II bVII IV V	4 bar cres. on V
Verse 4	2 bars	x 8	16	I IV V	
Prech.5	16 bars		16	IV III VI V	6 bar V cres.
Chorus3	2 bars	x 4	8	I IV V	
Link3	2 bars	x 4	8	[as chorus]	sax solo
Coda	2 bars	x 2	4	I IV V	b/v chant
	2 bars	x 4	8	I	as intro

■ 'Jungleland' (9:32), key C major

'Jungleland' is the epic finale to the *Born To Run* album. This song has carefully graded dynamics and instrumentation, opening with violins and piano. The first change of tempo is at 0:28. The song only turns into a full-blown rock number at 1:48 when the guitars and rhythm section enter. Everything builds the tension to this point.

The interesting thing about the structure of 'Jungleland' is that there is no return to the rock style that characterised verse 3 and following. Once the sax break comes in it slips into slower tempos and quieter dynamics. The song gets progressively slower and quieter. Key changes (discussed in Section 2) also play a role in creating contrasts between sections: it modulates flatward from C through F to D-flat, although it does make it back to C major at the start of the coda. Notice that drums and electric guitars are not heard in the last parts of the tune. There is no beat through much of the end and this gives the song a sense of anti-climax. Perhaps this made the track less of an obvious show-stopper live.

Section	Phrase	Repeats	Total	Chords	Notes
Intro	10 bars		10	I-VI incl.	strings, tempo 88
	2 bars	x 4	8	I IV V (C pedal)	piano, tempo 128
Verse 1	2 bars	x 6	12	I IV V	vocal in
	4 bars		4	II III IV V	
Link	2 bars	x 2	4	I IV V	(as intro)
Verse 2	2 bars	x 6	12	I IV V	
	4 bars		4	II III IV V	
Link 2	2 bars	x 2	4	I IV V	
Verse 3	2 bars	x 8	16	I IV V	band fully in
	2 bars	x 4	4	II III IV V	
	8 bars		8	bVII I II IV V	extension, hint of D minor
Link 2	2 bars	x 2	4	I IV V	
Solo 1	2 bars	x8	16	I IV V	(based on link) guitar
Bridge	8 bars	x 2	15	IV I V II (in F)	

[repeat loses 1 bar, bar 7]

Section	Phrase	Repeats	Total	Chords	Notes
Solo 2	14 bars		14	I IV bIII V (in Eb)	sax over maj7 + slash chords tempo down to 69
Solo 3	8 bars	x 3	24	I VI IV V (in Eb)	sax
Link 3	5 bars		5	bVII VI III ^ IV V	in Eb, piano
	8 bars		8	I VI IV V (in Eb)	as sax solo 2
Verse 4	8 bars	x 2	16	I VI IV V III ^	as sax solo 2

[the repeat changes the last two bars, tempo drops to 60]

Section	Phrase	Repeats	Total	Chords	Notes
	4 bars	x 4	16	II III IV V (in C)	as verse 3
	6 bars		6	bVII II IV V	extension, hint of D minor
Coda	12 bars		12	I VI V IV in C	tempo 144

■ New York City Serenade (9:44), key A major

If you write a long form song it doesn't have to replicate the complicated structures of the three previous numbers. You can take another route, which is to limit the musical material and create interest by the arrangement – which instruments play and when – and the dynamics.

There are several Springsteen songs that stretch a small amount of musical material over many minutes. They use dynamics (loud and soft) to sustain interest as opposed to throwing in extra chords, sequences, and key-changes.

The first example is the closing track of Springsteen's second album, 'New York City Serenade'. Like 'The Fever', it starts with a piano solo by David Sancious. The first effect heard is glissandi on the piano strings made by reaching inside the piano itself, which is 'intro 1'. This is followed by chords and arpeggios played conventionally for 'intro 2'. But the bulk of the song is a simple four-chord turnaround I-VI-II-IV in A major. The song ebbs and flows in terms of quiet passages and loud ones, with Springsteen adjusting his vocals from the almost whispered phrasing of the early sections to the passionate outbursts of the conclusion. Listen for Bridge 2, a dramatic switch of arrangement to piano, handclaps, and group vocals.

Section	Phrase	Repeats	Total	Chords	Notes
Intro 1	[free time piano effects]				
Intro 2				Ebm, Em, Am	Am key
Instr.verse	4 bars	x 2	8	I VI II IV	A major
Ac.gtr solo	4 bars	x 2	8		
Instr.verse	4 bars	x 2	8		
Verse	14 bars	x 4	16		tempo 82
Bridge	13 bars	-	13 (12+1)	ends 2 bars of V	
Link	4 bars	x 2	8		strings, perc. in
Verse 2	4 bars	x 8	32		sax heard
Bridge 2	4 bars	x 4	16	II VI	piano, claps
	4 bars	-	4	IV V	
Instr.verse	4 bars	x 2	8		
Verse 3	4 bars	x 2	8		cut short
Bridge 3	4 bars	x 2	8	II VI	pizz. strings
	4 bars	x 2	8	II IV	
	6 bars	-	6	V	build-up
Coda	4 bars	[ad lib to end]			dynamics vary

■ Drive All Night (8.26), key F major

If you want to be really daring you can always try to emulate the extreme economy that Bruce demonstrated in 'Drive All Night' (from *The River*). This number is a good example of getting as much from as little purely musical material as possible. The entire song is based on a two-bar, three-chord phrase that repeats for over eight minutes. The dynamics change and the instrumentation is varied to create the illusion of contrast. Some listeners feel that there isn't enough going on, and that it would have benefited from a different section somewhere to break the monotony of the two-bar phrase. Imagine that there were eight bars of different music before 'Drive All Night' reaches its "don't cry now" refrain, say where the link to the coda occurs. Now hear that lyric with the return of the three-chord change.

If you try this approach I recommend that you insert one section, perhaps about two-thirds or three-quarters of the way through, that makes a contrast with the dominant sequence. It could have some new chords, a new rate of chord change, a new time signature, or even be in a new key. It might even be only eight bars, but it will make the return of the main theme more powerful.

Section	Phrase	Repeats	Total	Chords	Notes
Intro	2 bars		2	I	bass and drum only
	2 bars	x 4	8	I IV V	piano enters
Verse 1	2 bars	x 4	8		vocal in
Chorus	2 bars	x 4	8		
Link	2 bars	x 2	4		organ, glock., gtr fill
Verse 2	2 bars	x 4	8		
Chorus 2	2 bars	x 4	8		bass fills
Sax solo	2 bars	x 8	16		strings, first cres.
Verse 2	2 bars	x 12	24		vocal cres.
Link	2 bars	x 2	4		much quieter, bv answer
Coda	2 bars	ad lib to fade	24		2nd cres.to fade, horns

◼ Land Of Hope And Dreams (9.12), key Bb major

Sometimes it is not easy to grasp how a song you have written actually has the potential to be more dramatic than it is in its current form. Such a song lengthens naturally when you realise that instead of having one climax, it can have many, and that you just need to stretch linking passages out a bit. As a result, your song could turn into a real asset for live performance. With more than one climax it can really engage the audience.

Springsteen is a master at seeing such a possibility. Included on the *Live In New York City* album, 'Land Of Hope And Dreams' sees him revisiting the long-form song and finding a new way of building multiple climaxes into it. Every time you think it may have ended it hasn't. The song strikes a good balance between the musical complexities of a structure like 'Rosalita' and the simplistic 'Drive All Night', and comes with a catchy mandolin-inspired riff. The Bb major key is made resonant and easy to play on the guitar by using a capo at the third fret, where Bb becomes a G shape.

Section	Phrase	Repeats	Total	Chords	Notes
Intro	4 bars		4	no chords	drums only
	4 bars	x 2	8	I IV	guitar, organ fills
	4 bars	x 2	8		band in; [link] riff
Verse 1	16 bars		16	I IV VI V	V also inverted
Chorus	6 bars		6	I IV VI V	
Link	4 bars	x 2	8		riff
Verse 2	16 bars		16		
Chorus2	6 bars		6		

continued on next page

Link 2	4 bars	x 2	8		riff
Bridge	8 bars	x 2	16	VI IV I IV	
Sax solo	4 bars	x 4	16		[link]
Bridge 2	8 bars	x 3	24		
Link 3	4 bars	x 2	8		riff
Bridge 3	8 bars	x 3	24		quieter, no dr/bs
Link 4	4 bars	x 2	8		riff
Link 5	4 bars	x 4	16		accented rhythm
Link 6	4 bars	x 2	8		riff
Coda	4 bars		4		accented rhythm
	[free time]	x 3		I VI IVIV	cres. on 'c'mon'

Technique summary

This first section has dealt with song structure and has shown you how to use the following songwriting techniques when you are mapping out your intro, verse, chorus or bridge:

- the 'false' intro;
- the recycled intro;
- the free time intro;
- the 8-bar form for a verse or chorus;
- the 12-bar form;
- the 'quick-change' 12-bar form;
- the four-chord non-blues 12-bar;
- the 16-bar form;
- the 'multiverse' extended verse form;
- the bridge / middle eight;
- the bridge that starts on chord IV;
- the bridge that starts on chord V;
- the '8+1' trick and other extended bridges;
- the complex long form song;
- the simple long form song.

So imagine you have your song structure. Now, what chords are you going to put in it? Which chords fit with each other? The chords will fill the verse and chorus; on them the melody and the words will ride. Section 2 will take you through tips and ideas drawn from Springsteen's use of common progressions and chords.

chords and sequences

THE TWO-CHORD SONG
'BORN IN THE USA'

It may seem counter-intuitive, but it's not easy to write a two-chord song. This is borne out by the fact that there are many more three-chord songs than two-chord songs. Fewer chords should be easier, but there's a hidden challenge. The two-chord song always runs the risk of monotony. The ear can tire of the pair of chords. The effect is curiously static, and can make the song feel as though it isn't going anywhere.

You can pick any two chords you like, but the the two likeliest pairs for two-chord songs are I and IV, or I and V. Here they are in the most popular guitar keys (most of these are easy open-string shapes):

Key	I	+	IV	[or]	I	+	V
F major	F		Bb		F		C
C major	C		F		C		G
G major	G		C		G		D
D major	D		G		D		A
A major	A		D		A		E
E major	E		A		E		B

A handful of two-chord songs in Springsteen's catalogue provide an example of how one famous songwriter approaches the problem. His emphasis on the lyric is certainly one way round it: if the listener is busy following the story of the words he or she may forget that there isn't more going on in the chords. 'The Big Muddy' is essentially I and IV, 'State Trooper' is I and IV played as fifths rather than full chords for a harder sound. 'Goin' Cali' is almost entirely E7 (ie, chord I), 'Lucky Man' is E or Em, with a suggestion of an A for the hook (I-IV).

Springsteen's stand-out two-chord song, by a long way, is 'Born In The USA'. It works because of the sheer power of its electric version, and the stark emotions evoked by the lyric and rousing chorus. Two-chord songs depend on how they are performed, arranged, and recorded. The E Street Band played with unparalleled ferocity and single-mindedness on this session.

'Born In The USA' started as an acoustic song during the *Nebraska* demo sessions. Drummer Max Weinberg described the way the song evolved and improved during the later session at which the E Street Band recorded it: "Bruce started playing this droning guitar sound. He threw that lick out to [keyboardists] Roy [Bittan] and Danny [Frederici], and the thing just fell together. It absolutely grabbed us. We played it again and got an even better groove on it. At the end as we were stopping, Bruce gave me the high sign to do all these wild fills, and we went back into the song and jammed for about ten minutes, which was edited out. I remember that night as the greatest single experience I've ever had recording, and it set the tone for the whole record."

Although the chords of 'Born In The USA' are B and E (I and IV) there's more to them than meets the ear. The B is played on the guitar as a droning B5. Both it and the E chord are coloured by the keyboard motif which is played over them. This motif adds harmonic interest by making the chords sound more complex than they are. The E chord comes out sounding like an Eadd9 because of the F# in the keyboard (Eadd9 = E G# B F#). Only at 4:09 is there a hint of chord V, a tentative F# in the bass, but neither the keyboards nor the guitars follow this.

If writing a two-chord song, there are techniques that will add interest:

• Consider varying the rate at which the chords change;
• Consider which chord is chosen to start the verse, chorus or bridge (if there is one);
• Play the chords also as first or second inversions, fifths (neither major nor minor), sus2s, sus4s, or as extended chords like sevenths or sixths. There is information about this in Section 4.

These options are explored in this song idea in G major, using only I and IV. The i or ii placed before a numeral indicates a first or second inversion.

Two-chord song in G major, I and IV

Intro

I				I				I				iI			
G5	/	/	/	G5	/	/	/	G5	/	/	/	G/B	/	/	/

Verse

IV				IV				I				I		iI	
C	/	/	/	C	/	/	/	G5	/	/	/	G5	/	G/B	/

IV				V				IV				I			
C5	/	/	/	C5	/	/	/	C	/	/	/	C	/	/	/

Chorus

I				iiI				IV				iIV			
G	/	/	/	G/D	/	/	/	C	/	/	/	C/E	/	/	/

Bridge

IV			iI		IV				I		iI	
C	/	Cmaj7	/	G/B	/	/	/	C	/	Cmaj7	/	G	/	G/B	/

IV				I				I				iiI			
C	/	/	/	G	/	Gmaj7	/	Gmaj7	/	/	/	G/D	/	/	/

Notice that:

- The intro only uses I.
- The verse brings in IV.
- The full root position G major is saved to the chorus.
- The bridge varies the rate of chord change to a chord every two beats.
- The bridge brings in the 'softer' major seventh chords.

THE I-VI AND I-IV CHANGE
'TENTH AVENUE FREEZE-OUT', 'BACKSTREETS', 'STREETS OF FIRE'

Although it is unlikely to be used through a whole song, there is another two-chord change that is central to songwriting which you can use throughout a song section. This change is from chord I to one of the minor chords that feature in every major key: chords II, III or VI. Here they are in the popular guitar keys.

Key	I	II	III	VI
F major	F	Gm	Am	Dm
C major	C	Dm	Em	Am
G major	G	Am	Bm	Em
D major	D	Em	F#m	Bm
A major	A	Bm	C#m	F#m
E major	E	F#m	G#m	C#m

Of the three, the I-VI change is the most significant. These two chords have a close affinity, with two out of three notes in common: if I is C major (C E G), VI will be A minor (A C E). A minor is the *relative minor* of C major; C major is the *relative major* of A minor.

Chords I-VI are related but express the fundamental change of going from major (a happy chord) to minor (a sad chord). This simple change can be dramatic when presented with the power of a rock band.

The major key has two other pairs of chords that are relative to each other in the same way as I and VI. In C major, chord II is D minor and its relative major is F (chord IV); Chord III is E minor and its relative major is G (chord V). So IV-II and V-III are major/minor changes in the same way as I-VI. Your song can use any or all of these changes, as these examples illustrate:

8-bar verse, relative majors to minors

I				VI				I				VI			
C	/	/	/	Am	/	/	/	C	/	/	/	Am	/	/	/

IV				II				IV				II			
F	/	/	/	Dm	/	/	/	F	/	/	/	Dm	/	/	/

There are many examples of the I-VI change in Springsteen's songs. 'Fire' starts with an implied I-VI change in G. 'Counting On A Miracle' starts its verse with I-VI in A, and continues the verse with II-IV. 'You're Missing' has an intro and much of its verse built on I-VI in F. 'Two Faces' has a verse built on I-VI in A. There's a I-VI change on the intro of 'Loose Ends' in G, and for the first four bars of the verse, for the link after chorus 1, and under the singing of the title in the coda to the fade.

The three songs whose titles appear above have their identity grounded in the I-VI change. 'Tenth Avenue Freeze-Out' has I-VI (F-Dm) as the main change for the intro and much of its verse, with IV-II supplementing. The verse and chorus of 'Streets Of Fire' feature a powerfully accented I-VI in A.

Using a pedal note

Simple changes like I-VI can be given an interesting twist by putting them over a pedal note. A pedal note is a note that stays static in the bass instead of changing with the chords. Pedal notes enable you to get more from a chord change like I-VI because it can be 'suspended' over the pedal first, and then heard with its proper changing bass root notes later on in the song. This is a good technique for an intro, which is how Springsteen arranged it on 'Backstreets'. This song starts its initial guitar riff and verse with I-VI in G, after a piano intro where the I-VI change is repeated over a pedal note G.

THE THREE-CHORD TRICK
'INDEPENDENCE DAY', 'MY LOVE WILL NOT LET YOU DOWN'

Two-chord songs are not that common, but millions of songs have been written with only three chords. Here's the simplest of song fragments using three chords; repeated four times it might make a verse or a chorus.

2-bar three-chord idea in G

I		IV	V				x4
G	/	C	/	D	/	/	/	:

The three 'magic' chords occur on the first, fourth and fifth notes of the scale. These chords can be described as I, IV and V regardless of their *pitch* name (A, C, D, F# etc). Here they are in the guitar-friendly keys:

Key	I	IV	V
F major	F	Bb	C
C major	C	F	G
G major	G	C	D
D major	D	G	A
A major	A	D	E
E major	E	A	B

We've already considered the I-IV and I-VI changes. Chord V creates a strong feeling of an imminent 'return home' whenever it is placed before chord I. A songwriter respects these two mighty players I and V in the musical system. One of the subtleties of songwriting is knowing where to place these chords, when to hold them back, when to stop them coming into contact, and how to arouse certain moods by their careful positioning. Chord IV isn't quite such a stabilising force as chord V, but still important for supporting the scale and key. In some contexts it offers a softer effect than chord V, as we saw when talking about middle eights. So the three work together beautifully, with the result a secure musical architecture to support the most varied of musical and lyric intentions.

Try playing these next examples to get the hang of the 'three chord trick', as it is popularly known.

8-bar three-chord trick verse and chorus in G major

I	I	V	IV
G / / /	G / / /	D / / /	C / / /

I	V	I	I
G / / /	D / / /	D / / /	C / / /

[chorus]

I	IV	IV	V
G / / /	C / / /	C / / /	D / / /

I	IV	V	V
G / / /	C / / /	D / / /	D / / /

Springsteen has written many three-chord songs, later rather than earlier in his career – partly because of the expansion of his musical style to take in a folk/country influence. Among his three-chord tricks are 'Nebraska', 'Mansion On The Hill', 'Highway Patroller', 'Used Cars', (all in D-flat); 'Sinaloa Cowboys', 'Across The Border' 'Johnny 99' (all in Bb); 'Reason To Believe', 'Independence Day', 'No Surrender' (all in F); 'Dry Lightning', 'My Best Was Never Good Enough', 'My Love Will Not Let You Down', 'Two Hearts' (all in C); 'County Fair', 'Cadillac Ranch' (both in G); 'The New Timer', 'Galveston Bay', '57 Channels (And Nothing On)' (all in D); 'Glory Days', 'Book Of Dreams' (both in A); 'Johnny Bye Bye', 'Shut Out The Light', and 'Cross My Heart' (all in E).

Three chords, three sections

The distribution of the three chords within the song's sections can be anything you like. Try any of these in your songs:

- Verse is chord I only, IV and V enter on the chorus;
- Verse is chords I and IV, V enters on the chorus;
- Verse is chords I and V, IV enters on chorus;
- Verse is chords I and V, IV enters on the bridge;
- Verse and chorus use I, IV and V; bridge has IV and V only.

Springsteen has used a variety of ideas in this respect: 'No Surrender' (F) uses all three chords in an 8t-bar verse and an 8-bar chorus. 'Factory' (C) uses a single 8-bar sequence that spends much time on C rather than the F and G chords that make up the three chord trick; this suggests lack of movement – the monotony of the working life. 'All Or Nothing At All' confines itself to I and IV for its verse.

'Leavin' Train' relies on I for its verse, keeping IV and V for its chorus. 'This Hard Land' has a three chord trick verse in G, adding extra colour with a Gsus4 chord (a variation of I), a G/B (a first inversion of I), and a Cadd9 (a variation of chord IV). Despite the variations it is still a three-chord song.

Extend your three chords

Remember that the three major chords of this type of song do not have to be only played in their simplest three-note form. You can turn them into inversions, sixths, sevenths, etc. For an example of how the major 7th chord can intensify the emotion of a three-chord song, take 'Something In The Night'. It turns its chord IV C into a Cmaj7 (the first chord you hear on the track). The chord change I-Imaj7-IV (in C: C-Cmaj7-F) features in 'Happy' (in Db) and in 'Linda Let Me Be The One' (in G, with chord V tacked on) on the chorus. The chord change of Imaj7-IVmaj7 and then V (in C: C-Cmaj7-Fmaj7-G) is also a pleasing one. For another approach, keep these two maj7 chords for your bridge; let the rest of the song be straight majors.

Here's an example of a 16-bar three-chord trick verse:

16-bar three chord trick (with an inversion)

I				iiIV				I				I			
G	/	/	/	C/G	/	/	/	G	/	/	/	G	/	/	/

I				I				IV				IV			
G	/	/	/	G	/	/	/	C	/	/	/	C	/	/	/

I				I				IV				IV			
G	/	/	/	G	/	/	/	C	/	/	/	C	/	/	/

I				V				I				I		V	
G	/	/	/	D	/	/	/	G	/	/	/	G	/	D	/

The 'over-lap' three-chord trick

Here's a bit of a stretching of the category of the 'three-chord trick' … but what the hell! These labels are only there for descriptive convenience; this is art, not science!

If a song changes key up a tone (ie, going from C major to D major) one chord will be common to the two keys: C-F-G + D-G-A – the common 'over-lap' chord is G (see the entry on key-changing for more on this). I call this an 'over-lap' three-chord trick because considered as discreet sections, before and after the key-change, it is as if we have two three-chord tricks glued together, or over-laid. Obviously, this means five chords are actually used, but it's valid to think of it as an 'over-lap' three-chord trick.

Springsteen's 'The Ties That Bind' is mostly a three-chord trick in C but it adds two more chords (D and A) to become a three chord-trick in D when it changes key towards its last verse and chorus, thus illustrating the over-lap principle.

THE THREE CHORD TRICK WITHOUT V
'IF I SHOULD FALL BEHIND'

Although the classic three-chord trick uses chords I, IV and V, there are other possible combinations you can work with. The presumption is that chord I will be one of the three (if you omitted it the song might sound harmonically ambiguous and unsettled).

The other purely major three-chord trick is I-IV-bVII, which in C major would be C-F-Bb. This is easily confused with I-IV-V in F major (F-Bb-C) but it does exist as a musical entity in its own right. 'Souls of the Departed' is an instance from Springsteen's songs. The bVII chord, the 'mixolydian' song (of which this is an example) and minor key three-chord tricks are discussed later in this section.

You can write a three-chord song that links chord I with any two of the other five chords (II, III, IV, V, or VI). Springsteen is attracted to the softening effect that happens in a ballad when chord V is replaced by VI, giving a I-IV-VI three-chord trick (in C major: C F Am). He does this for 'Highway 29' and memorably on 'If I Should Fall Behind'. There are numerous songs about the difficulties and disappointments of love, but considerably fewer which convincingly describe the time when romantic dreaming stops and the process of really loving begins. 'If I Should Fall Behind' is one of those.

The studio version has a quicker tempo (110 bpm) than the live, with a country-ish backbeat, synth pad, and acoustic guitars. Understated and workmanlike, it doesn't quite get to grips with the emotion of the song. Springsteen obviously felt he could get more from it, remodelling it for the *MTV Plugged* show by changing the key from D to E major and slowing the tempo to 102. He sings the first verse with no percussion, just guitar and a synth. Verse 2 brings in the rest of the band and the last verse has the populist touch of mandolin-type strumming. The drums fall out for the last verse and re-enter for a repeat of the last lines. The live version puts a harmonica break before the bridge and that's where you feel the difference in emotional depth. In concert, the song later became an important moment for The E Street Band to step forward as individuals, as can be heard on *Live In New York City*.

Here's an example of a similar three-chord trick with I, II and IV. Notice the use of an inversion, varied rate of chord change, and the withholding of Dm to the chorus.

8-bar three-chord song, I-II-IV in C major

I	I	iiIV	I
C / / /	C / / /	F/C / / /	C / / /

iiIV	I	I	iiIV	I
F/C / / /	C / / /	C /	F/C /	C / / /

[chorus]

I	IV	II	IV	I	I
C /	F /	Dm /	F /	C / / /	C / / /

[bridge]

II	II	I	II	II	I
Dm / / /	Dm /	C /	Dm / / /	Dm /	C /

II	II	IV	IV
Dm / / /	Dm / / /	F / / /	F / / /

DISPLACING AND WITHHOLDING CHORDS
'PROVE IT ALL NIGHT', 'DANCING IN THE DARK', 'MY BEAUTIFUL REWARD'

Displacing or withholding a chord are two techniques applicable to any chord progression no matter how many chords are in it, but the techniques are especially important in three- or four-chord songs. Your songs will gain in artistry if you can master this principle.

Displacing a chord

This simply means moving a chord to a position that reduces, relatively, its influence over the sequence. It's like turning the light off above a picture on a gallery wall: you can still see it but the illuminated paintings either side stand out more. The chord most likely to be displaced is chord I.

Chord I is the most stable, fixed point in a key's harmony. It is the place where things come to rest; symbolically, where questions are answered, where hopes are fulfilled, where things find their place.

If chord I starts a sequence the music begins on the point of balance. If it comes at the end there is a sense of order re-established. If a short musical sequence both begins and ends on chord I the progression asserts that everything in between is an in-control journey from order to order. Sometimes a songwriter needs to prevent chord I being in either of these positions to give the music more instability and flow. In the next example the influence of chord I (G) has been reduced:

Eight-bar verse in G major, displacing chord I

IV				V				IV				I			
C	/	/	/	D	/	/	/	C	/	/	/	G	/	/	/

V				I				V				IV			
D	/	/	/	G	/	/	/	D	/	/	/	C	/	/	/

It is a subtle difference, admittedly – there are only three chords in their simplest forms – but those three chords are the ones that most assert the feeling of a stable key.

In Springsteen's music, examples of this include 'Sad Eyes', where chord I (D) is constantly displaced in the verse and chorus, as many of the phrases start on IV and flow right on through chord I when it does occur. In the chorus of 'Into The Fire' chord I (F) is displaced in the repeated sequence of Bb-F/A-C-Bb; its first inversion (F/A) assists the displacement effect because a first inversion is less emphatic than a root chord.

Displacement plays a crucial role in 'My Beautiful Reward', in G with a hook-line that goes from D to G to C, with two bars on C to the one bar each that D and G get. The displacement produces a sense of unease. The displacement of chord I in 'One Step Up' is endemic, creating restlessness; the music never comes to rest but progresses backwards and forwards, appropriately for a lyric about a couple who can't move forward.

You can achieve displacement not only through the position of a chord but also by how many beats it occupies. 'Leap Of Faith' (in B) has a chorus progression of V-I-IV and a bridge that goes IV-V-I. In both cases the I is only played for two beats. The chorus of 'My Love Will Not Let You Down' displaces chord I into the middle of its V-V-IV-IV-I-I-IV-IV 8-bar sequence. 'Dancing In The Dark' displaces chord I during its middle-eight where the classic four-chord turnaround of I-IV-V-VI becomes VI-I-IV-V. This gives the song's middle-eight a more minor feel to contrast with the verse, dominated by chord I, and the chorus, which is dominated by chord V.

Withholding a chord

To withhold a chord means to put it aside and not bring it in until later in a song. This technique is only really effective with four chords, but it can still make a difference in a three-chord song.

Examples from Springsteen include 'Two Hearts', a three-chord trick in C which saves chord V for the chorus. 'My City Of Ruins' functions much of the time on a I-VI-IV-I looping sequence where chord V is withheld. 'Valentine's Day' has a verse based on I and IV, and a bridge that brings in VI and III, so V is avoided until the end of the bridge; the song expresses the longing of the singer musically by reducing the influence of chord V. 'Racing In The Street' has I-IV-VI-IV in F for its chorus and coda; this progression avoids chord V (C) which only briefly sounds in the piano intro and during a later link passage. Springsteen uses the same three chords for the verse of 'Nothing Man', withholding chord V for the chorus and the 'doo-doo' section. Chord I (A) is withheld from the chorus of 'It's Hard To Be A Saint In The City', and 'Prove It All Night' which relies on IV-V-VI and a chord III.

Substituting an inversion

One trick when withholding a chord is to substitute an inversion for its root form. In a three-chord trick each chord can occur in root, first or second inversion. In C major C, F, and G thus become C, C/E, C/G, F, F/A, F/C, G, G/B, G/D – nine chords from three.

A second inversion of chord IV has the same bass note as the root position of chord I. In C major iiIV is F/C and chord I has the root note C. This suggests the I-IV change without actually doing it. You can save an actual C-F chord change until later in your song, using C-F/C for the intro or the verse.

'Local Hero' is a three-chord trick in Bb where I goes to iiIV in the intro, chord IV being withheld to bar eight of the verse. Springsteen uses the I-iiIV change in many songs, whether ballads or uptempo rockers. For more on this see the entry on inversions in Section 4.

Chord I can also be withheld by turning it into a first inversion. In this example chord I's influence is reduced because in the verse it only appears once – as an inversion that lasts for two beats (not even at the start of a bar). Its root position is withheld until the chorus for impact.

8-bar verse, II-III-V in D major, withholding I

II	II	V	V	iI
Em / / /	Em / / /	A / / /	A /	D/F# /

II	II	IV	V
Em / / /	Em / / /	G / / /	A / / /

[chorus]

I	I	V	IV
D / / /	D / / /	A / / /	G / / / :

THE RATE OF CHORD CHANGE
'MY CITY OF RUINS', 'DOWNBOUND TRAIN', 'THE GHOST OF TOM JOAD'

Another technique for refining your chord sequence is to vary the rate of chord change. When putting a song together consider: how often do the chords change? Does a chord always occupy a whole bar? Ensuring that the rate at which your chords change is not always the same is a shield against monotony. The fewer chords in a song the more significant it is to have variety by means of a fluctuating rate of chord-change. It partly off-sets the lack of harmonic contrast. If the general rate of chord change is one chord to a bar, the most useful alternatives are to have:

- Two chords in a bar (change on beats 1 and 3, 1 and 4, or 1 and 2);
- One chord over a bar and a half;
- One chord over two bars;
- Four chords in a bar (change on each beat).

Here is a sequence where there are two chords in bar 4. This creates extra motion just where it might be handy, at the end of a phrase, and this idea is developed in bars 7-8 where it happens twice. Conversely, in bars 10-11 the music stays on a D chord for two bars. In bar 15 there is one chord on each beat.

12-bar verse in Em

I	III	VII	VI	VII
Em / / /	G / / /	D / / /	C /	D /

I	III	VI	VII	VI	III
Em / / /	G / / /	C /	D /	C /	G /

VII	VII	I	VII	VI	IV	V^
D / / /	D / / /	Em	D	C	Am	B7 / / / / :|

One-chord-to-a-beat can be dramatic. Done too often it will bewilder the listener, the more so the quicker the tempo. Rates of chord change that put different chords on adjacent beats are tempo-sensitive. Only at slower tempi does a listener have time to respond to the contrasts between the four chords. But four-chords-in-a-bar can add spice to a verse or bridge where the rate is otherwise one chord to a bar. It heightens the drama of transitions from one section to another.

There are significant rate-of-chord-change variations in some of Springsteen's songs. 'Dancing In The Dark' has a chord change every bar throughout its verse, which is 16 bars long. Chord V is withheld until the chorus, where we get four bars on the trot and no chord I in the chorus either. 'Downbound Train' has a 16-bar verse. Bars 1-4 repeat, then bars 5-6 set up an expectation of IV-V but by staying on V for bar 7 this is a surprise. 'My City Of Ruins' has mostly two-beat changes at a slow tempo but has one bar (first heard at the very start) where there is a different chord on each of the four beats, making an effective contrast.

Unpredictable rates of chord change lend authenticity to some of Springsteen's folkier songs, such as 'Galveston Bay', and 'The Ghost Of Tom Joad' where after four bars on Bm (chord I) and a bar on D there is a split bar of two beats D, two beats A, followed by four bars on A and then another split bar of Bm and A. This style accommodates irregular lyric lines and vocal pauses. Solo performers can do this because you don't have to worry about a band getting 'thrown' if you deviate from the strict rate of changes.

THE FOUR-CHORD SONG
'JACKSON CAGE', 'STOLEN CAR', 'ATLANTIC CITY'

If you feel confident with three-chord songs, or you want more chords to play with, you move up to the four-chord number. Along with the three-chord trick, the four-chord song is very popular. The usual choice is to add a minor chord – either II, III or VI – to the I, IV, V of the three-chord trick. Here are the relevant chords for the popular guitar keys.

Key	I	II	II	IV	V	VI
F major	F	Gm	Am	Bb	F	Dm
C major	C	Dm	Em	F	G	Am
G major	G	Am	Bm	C	D	Em
D major	D	Em	F#m	G	A	Bm
A major	A	Bm	C#m	D	E	F#m
E major	E	F#m	G#m	A	B	C#m

II, III and VI are all minor chords, so the opportunity to add a minor chord provides significant new 'colour' in the palette of harmony. This in turn brings new inspiration to a familiar structure such as a 12-bar:

12-bar verse in E, chords I-III-IV-V

I				I				I				I			
E	/	/	/	E	/	/	/	E	/	/	/	E	/	/	/

I				IV				III				III			
A	/	/	/	A	/	/	/	G#m	/	/	/	G#m	/	/	/

IV				V				I				I			
A	/	/	/	B	/	/	/	E	/	/	/	E	/	/	/

There are three primary four-chord combinations: I-IV-V-VI; I-II-IV-V; and I-III-IV-V. The four chords chosen can be put in any order. Try these out first; you will find they lend themselves to choruses very easily.

The I-IV-V-VI group

The first of these three combinations has informed many Springsteen songs. This chord combination is found in 'Atlantic City' (in Ab); 'Balboa Park' (in Bb), and 'The Rising' (in Bb) where VI is saved to the guitar solo; 'You're Missing', and 'Tougher Than The Rest' (both in F), which keeps VI until the bridge where it is the first chord; 'The Line' (in C), 'Darlington County' (in C), with the chorus using IV and V only, 'You Can Look But You Better Not Touch' (in C) where IV, V and VI are saved for the chorus, 'Secret Garden' (in C); 'I Wish I Were Blind' (G), 'Two For The Road' (G), 'My Beautiful Reward' (in G), keeping VI for the second verse, and 'All That Heaven Will Allow' (in G) keeping VI for the bridge.

Other Springsteen songs that use it are 'Where The Bands Are' (in D) where the four chords make its verse, 'Straight Time' (in D); 'Car Wash', 'My Hometown', 'Wreck On The Highway' (all in A); 'Janey Don't You Lose Heart', 'Jackson Cage', 'I'm On Fire', 'Crush On You', 'Sad Eyes' (all in E), 'Badlands' (also in E), where VI is saved until the chorus. Re-arranged as I-VI-IV-V (in G) it forms the foundation for the guitar and sax solos on 'The Promised Land'.

The I-II-IV-V group

Less favoured by Springsteen, this combination is nevertheless found in 'Living Proof' (in D), where chord II is saved to the bridge; 'The Promise' and 'Sherry Darling' (both F), and 'Brothers Under The Bridge ('83)' (in A).

A complete four-chord song

Let's now lay out a complete song structure that uses four chords, one of which is minor. The key is D major. A three-chord trick song in D would have the chords D, G and A. To those three let's add one minor – chord II, which is Em.

You would then decide how many verses, choruses and bridges your song needed.

Verse/bridge four-chord song in D major

Intro

V	V	V	IV
A / / /	A / / /	A / / /	G / / / ‖

Verse

I	IV	V	I
D / / /	G / / /	A / / /	D / / /
IV	**IV**	**V**	**iiV**
G / / /	G / / /	A / / /	A/E / / /

II	IV	I	V
Em / / /	G / / /	D / / /	A / / / ‖

Bridge

IV	IV	IV　　V	IV
G / / /	G / / /	G / A /	G / / /

IV	IV	II	V
G / / /	G / / /	Em / / /	A / / /

How often the minor chord occurs will affect how much of an impression it makes when you do use it. In this connection it is worth mentioning 'Stolen Car'. In the version released on *The River* the song mostly consists of a two-chord change from G to C, with the C sometimes substituted by a C/G inversion chord. After the vocal has ended and the instrumental coda is underway, shortly before the fade-out, the piano leads a sudden shift in the rate of chord change.

Chord V (D) is heard and a devastating first use of chord VI (Em) which seems to release all the gloom and despair from the singer's heart like a bottle of ink spilled into a vase of water.

THE FOUR-CHORD TURNAROUND
'HUNGRY HEART', 'NOTHING MAN', 'BECAUSE THE NIGHT'

Beyond the fact of a song using four chords, there is a specific way to treat those four chords which is an important songwriting technique. This is the 'turnaround'.

For good or ill, once you know about turnarounds your songwriting will never be the same again!

The turnaround is a chord pattern, usually two or four bars long, fixed by repetition. It is a progression that loops, literally 'turns around', many times. Repetition makes a turnaround what it is.

It often forms the 'hookiest' point of a song. Four-chord turnarounds gain their power not only from the increase of harmonic colour that a fourth (especially minor) chord brings. It is also that they take on an assertive symmetry, because of the number four. Many turnarounds are four chords, four beats each, in a four-bar phrase … that may even be repeated four times!

The primary, or 'Big Three', of turnarounds are those that use the three major chords with one of the three minors: I-II-IV-V, I-III-IV-V or I-VI-IV-V. Here they are in the keys of G and D:

Primary four-chord turnarounds in G

I				II				IV				V			
G	/	/	/	Am	/	/	/	C	/	/	/	D	/	/	/ :||

I				III				IV				V			
G	/	/	/	Bm	/	/	/	C	/	/	/	D	/	/	/ :||

I				VI				IV				V			
G	/	/	/	Em	/	/	/	C	/	/	/	D	/	/	/ :||

Primary four-chord turnarounds in D

I				II				IV				V			
D	/	/	/	Em	/	/	/	G	/	/	/	A	/	/	/ :||

I				III				IV				V			
D	/	/	/	F#m	/	/	/	G	/	/	/	A	/	/	/ :||

I				VI				IV				V			
D	/	/	/	Bm	/	/	/	G	/	/	/	A	/	/	/ :||

If ideas for a song hook have suddenly hit you after playing these, I'm not surprised. The examples can be re-arranged into any sequence of the four chords.

To be a turnaround the important thing is that the sequence is repeated often enough to form a harmonic and rhythmic unit which feels like a single object.

For a different approach, note that a *four*-bar turnaround can be made with only *three* chords simply by repeating one or more of the chords. As long as the sequence has a certain balance, and is repeated, it still works.

Springsteen does not make as much use of turnarounds as some people. Probably the two most striking examples in his catalogue are 'Hungry Heart', where the turnaround is the four-bar sequence I-VI-II-V (in C) which drives the entire song (along with a key-change), and 'Because The Night', whose chorus is a good example of a three-chord turnaround (I-VI-VII in B minor), a turnaround that is also the first part of the verse with a different rhythm. Remember from the long form songs of Section 1 that 'Drive All Night' has a two-bar turnaround for its entire length, and 'New York City Serenade' has a I-VI-II-IV turnaround in A for much of its structure.

You can create other variations by shuffling the order of the two internal chords in the turnaround. The primary group I-IV-V-VI is re-jigged to a I-V-VI-IV turnaround in Bb in 'I'm Goin' Down' and as I-VI-V-IV in A for parts of 'American Skin (41 Shots)'. 'Nothing Man' arranges the same chords as I-V-IV-VI-V (with the last two chords as a shared bar). I-V-II-IV is the turnaround in D for 'Bring On The Night', and IV-I-VI-III is the plunging minor turnaround in the chorus of 'Happy', a sequence whose dark power threatens to undermine the sentiment of the lyric. 'Waiting On A Sunny Day' has a three-chord but four bar I-VI-IV-I turnaround.

The 'escalator' effect

The 'escalator' effect is what happens when a sequence puts chords in numerical order. Going I-IV-V creates the feeling of ascending – as if on an escalator – while V-IV-I does the reverse:

Rising 'escalator'

I				I				IV				V			
G	/	/	/	G	/	/	/	C	/	/	/	D	/	/	/

Descending 'escalator'

V				IV				I				I			
D	/	/	/	C	/	/	/	G	/	/	/	G	/	/	/

The 'escalator' effect is more pronounced if four or five chords are involved. Then it has a natural affinity with the prechorus, where the effect heightens the expectation of the chorus's imminent arrival. The 'escalator' effect gives a chord progression a powerful feeling of literally that, *progression* – going towards something, ie, towards chord I or chord V. The most famous escalator (and this could be a turnaround if it is repeated enough) is one associated with 1960s Motown, which makes a classic approach to a chorus. Here it is in C:

Classic prechorus 'escalator'

II	III	IV	V
Dm / / /	Em / / /	F / / /	G / / /

There's an escalator like this in 'Jungleland', 'Bring On The Night', and, from the timing 2:04, in Springsteen's 'Seaside Bar Song'.

A further refinement is to repeat the first bit of the escalator to delay the final one or two chords. This technique lends itself to the crowd-teasing build-ups and climaxes which Springsteen wired into his early music with such great effect:

Stretched 'escalator'

II	III	(x3) IV	V
Dm / / /	Em / / / :‖	F / / /	G / / /

This sequence lasts 8 bars in all. The Dm-Em change happens three times before chord IV and V are heard. Springsteen's recent 'Let's Be Friends' (which has something of Smokey Robinson about it) has a stretched escalator in it, functioning as a prechorus.

THE FIVE-AND SIX-CHORD SONG
'BLINDED BY THE LIGHT', 'THE PROMISED LAND', 'HEARTS OF STONE'

Moving beyond three- and four-chord songs, you enter the realm of using five or six chords. The musical possibilities now greatly increase. Reflect on this for a second …

Each of these six chords has two inversions plus the root chord – which gives 18 available chords! Each chord can be coloured as a 7th , an add9, a sus4 or sus2. With all this harmonic material, writing chorus turnarounds that have mostly different chords to the verse, for example, is easy. If you vary the rate of chord change, five or even six chords will fit in four bars and make a turnaround.

If you're stuck for a selection of chords, how about these. Here are some of the five-chord combinations in Springsteen (these are not turn-arounds): 'Hearts Of Stone' (in F) uses I, IV and V in the chorus, I III IV V and VI in the verse; 'Streets Of Philadelphia' is the same six chords in F and 'Growin' Up' uses I II IV V VI in C; 'So Young And In Love' (holds II back for the bridge) and 'The Promised Land' use I II IV V VI in G; 'Loose Ends' uses I II IV V VI in G; 'The Price You Pay' in G uses I III IV V for most of the song but there's a VI brought in near the end for the line before "I'm gonna take it all and throw it away"; 'Better Days' is I II IV V VI in D; 'I Wanna Marry You' (in D) is I III IV V VI, keeping the two minor chords for the bridge; 'Not Fade Away' (in D) is mostly a three-chord trick on I IV V but the organ solo brings in VI and II; 'Blinded By The Light' has I II IV V VI in E – it does the verse on I and IV only, the chorus brings in the other three chords; 'Dancing In The Dark' is in B with I II IV V VI.

Springsteen's six-chord songs include some mentioned later under key-changes, though there is a difference between these and a song that uses six chords in a single key. The proper six-chorders (with chords I-VI) include: 'Thunder Road', 'Man's Job', 'For You' (all in F); 'Does This Bus Stop At 82nd Street?' and 'Give The Girl A Kiss' in G; 'Mary Queen Of Arkansas' in D (II is held back for the bridge at 2:47 and 2:53); 'Prove It All Night' in A; 'She's The One' in E. The middle-eight/sax solo of 'Mary's Place' uses II, III and VI in F; the all-minor feel contrasts with the rest of the song.

Here's an example for you to play for a song that has six chords:

Full song in A, six chords

Intro

III				III				II				II			
C#m	/	/	/	C#m	/	/	/	Bm	/	/	/	Bm	/	/	/

Verse

V				I				IV		I		IV		V	
E	/	/	/	A	/	/	/	D	/	A	/	D	/	E	/

IV				V				III				IV		V	
D	/	/	/	E	/	/	/	C#m	/	/	/	D	/	E	/

Chorus

I				V				VI				IV			
A	/	/	/	E	/	/	/	F#m	/	/	/	D	/	/	/

Bridge

II				II				II				IV			
Bm	/	/	/	Bm	/	/	/	Bm	/	/	/	D	/	/	/

II				II				II		IV		V		IV	
Bm	/	/	/	Bm	/	/	/	Bm	/	D	/	E	/	D	/

THE 'MIXOLYDIAN SONG'

By this stage you may be asking whether there can be more than six chords in a key? To which the answer is yes.

There is in fact a chord VII. Unlike the other six, it is neither major nor minor but diminished. You don't need to worry now about the theoretical reason for this. Suffice to say that the diminished chord is rarely found in songs. It is unsettling, hard to finger on the guitar, and hard to sing over … and generally not very rock'n'roll! So you can pretty much forget it.

Instead, the approach to chord VII relevant for songwriting lies with this simple formula: take the 7th degree of a major scale, lower it by a semi-tone, and treat that note as the root of a major chord. This makes a chord numbered bVII, the 'b' indicating that it is built on a lowered degree of the scale. In C this bVII chord would be Bb. There is a scale called the mixolydian mode, which is the major scale with a lowered 7th note (C D E F G A Bb instead of C D E F G A B). The term 'mixolydian song' serves as shorthand to describe a song that brings in the bVII, or turns chord V into a minor (another harmony consequence of the lowered 7th), though this is rarer.

You can have a mixolydian three-chord trick with I-IV-bVII or I-V-bVII. This can give songs a hard, bluesy sound if played with aggression. 'Trouble River' is a three-chord song in which E goes to F# repeatedly. F# has to be the key, the third chord being B and the E a bVII – so it's a mixolydian three-chord trick. 'Cynthia' has I bVII IV for most of its verse in D. 'Iceman' uses this change in Eb in its verse.

Mixolydian harmony arises when the bVII is added to chords I-VI inclusive. So in G this would mean writing a song with chords G Am Bm C D Em F, as Springsteen did when he wrote 'The Angel'. 'Spare Parts' uses the bVII in its verse. The middle-eight of 'Tenth Avenue Freeze-Out' has an Eb which is the bVII of F. The sax solo bridge of 'Lion's Den' has the Bb which is the bVII of C. There's a bVII of the key of G (an F) in 'Wild Billy's Circus Story' at 3:05 on the word "small". 'Human Touch' has a I IV bVII verse in G, the middle-eight brings in an Am, and the chorus goes IV-bVII which sounds like the music has changed key to C. 'It's Hard To Be A Saint In The City' has a bVII on its intro and during links. 'Real World' in Bb uses I IV V and bVII.

The presence of the bVII chord sometimes leads to uncertainty as to which key the music is in. The mixolydian three-chord trick in C (C-Bb-F) happens to be the same chords as a I-IV-V in F (F-Bb-C). Things get even more uncertain if chord V is turned into a minor. This happens in the verse and chorus of 'The Fuse', which has the chords D Am C and G) in D, where C is the bVII and Am the V in a minor form. Another instance would be 'Real Man', which is in B. It has the bVII (A) and the V as a minor (F#m) and there's a lot of bVII-I on the coda and throughout. 'Darkness On The Edge of Town is mostly I IV V VI in G, but it does smuggle in V as a minor (Dm) for the hook phrase "edge of".

The classic case of this ambiguity is 'Tunnel Of Love', much of which is a turnaround of C Gm Bb and F. By strict textbook rules this should be V-II-IV-I in F major, and it is true that the track comes in on F. However, the C chord insists on its primacy at the start of each sequence and comes to sound like the key chord. To test this, try imagining an ending somewhere in the middle of the song. C fits much better than F. The track's final seconds do not resolve the issue because it's a fade, though it is interesting that the last chord heard is not an F, as if they didn't think that was the home chord either when they mixed it.

As a songwriter you don't have to lose sleep over this. If it sounds good, that's what counts.

CHROMATIC AND UNEXPECTED CHORDS
'BOBBY JEAN', 'I'M A ROCKER', 'OUT ON THE STREETS'

You will be intrigued, and possibly excited, to know that being the wily non-conforming folk they are, songwriters sometimes put chords in a song that strictly don't belong in the key. These so-called 'chromatic' and altered chords are more characteristic of jazz than rock, so it is not surprising that there aren't many examples in Springsteen's music. His most colourful (the literal meaning of 'chromatic') songs in harmony terms are those with a jazz influence, such as 'The Fever', 'Frontline', 'New York City Serenade', and 'Meeting Across The River'. It makes one regret that Springsteen never made an album of similarly jazz-influenced songs, where his powerful narrative lyrics could have a rich harmonic setting.

Turning minors into majors

One type of altered chord arises when chords II, III or VI are turned into majors (indicated by a ^ next to the Roman numeral). In my book *How To Write Songs On Guitar*, I gave these the name of 'reverse polarity' chords – the 'polarity' being whether they were major or minor.

Springsteen turns II into a major in 'Bobby Jean' (in A) which has a B (II^) as the last two bars of its eight-bar verse. This altered chord, from minor to major, is crucial to the generosity of the song's sentiment. 'Bobby Jean' has I II^ III IV VI. 'I'm A Rocker' features the same chord in the same key at the end of its verse. 'I Wanna Be With You' uses I IV and V on the chorus, saves II^ and VI for the prechorus. 'Give The Girl A Kiss' also has a II^. Belying the populist tone of its lyric, 'Out On The Streets' includes I II III^ IV V VI and bVII – A Bm C# D E F#m and G – making it harmonically one of Springsteen's more adventurous songs.

'Lowered degree' chords

Another type of altered chord occurs when you lower a chord by a semitone and turn it into a major if it wasn't already a major. This happens with III which becomes bIII (in C major: Em to Eb), and VI which becomes bVI (Am to Ab).

A couple of Springsteen songs provide examples. There's a bVI-V (Ab-G) change in C major at the end of the verse of 'The E Street Shuffle' on the word "doing". The Db (a bVI) toward the end of 'Night' (2:32, just before "you run sad and free") is a surprise. The music hangs on this chord with a mild feeling of shock. The bVII chord is sometimes paired with the bIII. 'When The Lights Go Out' has a bIII and bVII in F#. The bIII chord appears in 'Gloria's Eyes' which is in A – the bIII chord is Cadd9 and you can hear it under the guitar solo changing to a IV. 'Candy's Room' has a beautiful bIII-II-I change in G major at 2:33-37, where the bIII is unexpected.

Chromatic build-ups

If you want to create excitement when going from one section of a song to another, try moving a major chord up in semitones toward the first chord of the next section.

Springsteen made use of chromatic chord movement by semitones to heighten the build-up during a transition from one section to another. 'Kitty's Back' has a chromatic chord passage at 3:10-34 with an anarchic jazz feel. 'Rosalita' has its chromatic passage at 3:18-42 where the music edges up a semitone at a time from C to E as it builds to the sax bridge. The most effective use of semitone chord movement in Springsteen is of course in 'Born To Run', at the end of the guitar break (2:50-59), where the music slides from F through F# up to A# before descending by semitones through all 12 major chords from B down to B in preparation for the dramatic return to E major at the last verse.

Here's an example of a chromatic bridge. To increase the expectation of the D chord that will follow the bridge, the rate of chord change increases in the last few bars.

Chromatic bridge in Dmajor

I				bII				II^				bIII			
A	/	/	/	Bb	/	/	/	B	/	/	/	C	/	/	/

III^				IV		bV		V		bVI		VI^		bVII	
C#	/	/	/	D	/	Eb	/	E	/	F	/	F#	/	G	/

THE LAST CHORD
'MY CITY OF RUINS', 'EMPTY SKY', 'GROWIN' UP'

How are you going to end your song?

Assuming your song doesn't fade out, it will have a final chord. This chord is expected to be the key chord, chord I, to bring the song to a conclusion. Dynamics and instrumentation also have a bearing on a song's ending. But some songs don't want to end on chord I, either because of their mood or the lyric's theme. It doesn't make much sense for a song about uncertainty or a lack of fulfilment to end with the certainty and fulfilment of the key chord. Lyric content can make ending on chord I a false consolation.

So what are the options? If you want to, how do you make a song end less securely? After chord I, the next likeliest final chords would be IV or V.

Chord IV gives a song a less secure end than chord I, whilst still remaining positive. It leaves things mildly unresolved but not unhappily so. Sometimes it is like a question mark hanging in the air. Examples of Springsteen songs that end on IV include 'Lonesome Day', 'The Rising', 'For You', 'New York City Serenade', and 'American Skin (41 Shots)'. On *Live In New York City*, 'Murder Incorporated' ends on a IV^ in E minor (A) and holds it to land on E as chord I of the next song, 'Badlands'. Chord IV can be given extra romanticism if turned into a major7, as in 'My City Of Ruins', which ends on Ebmaj7.

Springsteen songs which end on chord V include 'Growin' Up', whose last chord is G in the key of C, and 'The Angel', whose last chord is D in the key of G. Further afield, there is 'Counting On A Miracle' which ends on G, the bVII of the home key A. If you consider 'Lost In The Flood' to be in E minor then it ends on VII, D; 'Empty Sky' is in G minor but ends on the VII chord, F. The version of 'Incident on 57th Street' on *Live in Barcelona* ends on chord V.

Ending a major-key song on any of its three minor chords can be chilling, like putting a foot into bathwater and finding it's freezing cold. Springsteen elects to end with a minor on the *Live in Barcelona* 'Prove It All Night', which finishes on chord VI (F#m) – although the song then segues into the next. If a song is in a minor key (see below) there is a well-known trick of turning the final chord I to the tonic major for unexpected brightness; a song in A minor thus ends on an A major chord.

Here are some sample endings:

Ending in G major on chord IV

I				I		II		IV				V			IV	
G	/	/	/	G	/	Am	/	C	/	/	/	D7sus4 /	D7	/	C(maj7)	

Ending in G major on chord V

I				I		II		IV				VI			V	
G	/	/	/	G	/	Am	/	C	/	/	/	Em	/	/	D	

Ending in G major on chord II

I				I		II		IV				V			II	
G	/	/	/	G	/	Am	/	C	/	/	/	D7sus4 /	D7	/	Am	

Ending in G major using chord IVm

I				I		II		IV				IVm		I		
G	/	/	/	G	/	Am	/	C	/	/	/	Cm	/	/	G	

Ending in G minor on chord VII

I				I		III		VI				I		VI		VII
Gm	/	/	/	Gm	Bb	/	Eb	/	/	/	Gm	Eb	/	F		

THE MINOR KEY SONG
'POINT BLANK', 'MURDER INCORPORATED'

Most of the songs discussed so far have been major key songs. But you can write a song in a minor key. Springsteen, like most songwriters, has done this from time to time. The way chords line up in a minor key is slightly more complicated than with the major key. This is because there is more than one type of minor scale from which the chords are derived. Putting theory aside, use this model I devised, which I call the songwriter's composite minor key. Here is it for the three most common minor keys on the guitar:

Composite A minor

I	III	IV	(IV$^\wedge$)	V	(Vm)	VI	VII
Am	C	Dm	(D)	E	(Em)	F	G

Composite D minor

I	III	IV	(IV$^\wedge$)	V	(Vm)	VI	VII
Dm	F	Gm	(G)	A	Am	Bb	C

Composite E minor

I	III	IV	(IV$^\wedge$)	V	(Vm)	VI	VII
Em	G	Am	(A)	B	(Bm)	C	D

These are the chords you would choose from if you were writing a song in A minor, D minor or E minor.

The chords in brackets are alternative major or minor chords for that degree of the scale. A two-chord A minor key song could be I-IVm (Am-Dm) or I-IV$^\wedge$ (Am-D); a minor three-chord trick could be I-IV-V (Am-Dm-E), I-IV$^\wedge$-V (Am-D-E), I-IV-Vm (Am-Dm-Em), or I-IV$^\wedge$-Vm (Am-D-Em). The I-VII-VI (Am-G-F) is a hugely popular chord sequence. For a four-chord minor key song, the sequences I-III-IV-V, I-III-IV-VI or I-VII-VI-V (or Vm) have been used countless times.

Among Springsteen's minor-key songs, 'Seeds' gets by with an Em-based riff with chord IV$^\wedge$ (A) coming in only at the end. Chords I, VI and VII are the basis for 'Paradise' (in C minor) and 'Empty Sky'(in G minor); 'Worlds Apart' is in E minor, mainly built on I, III and VII; 'Youngstown' has I, III and VII in D minor. 'Part Man Part Monkey' (C minor) uses a ska rhythm, a 12-bar structure, and chords I, IV and V. Among the four-chord songs, 'Lucky Town' and 'Downbound Train' (both G minor) use I, III, VI, and VII (Gm, Bb, Eb, F); 'The Ghost Of Tom Joad' is the same in B minor.

Of the five-chord songs, 'Adam Raised A Cain' (in E minor) has I, III, IV, V, and VI; 'Further On (Up The Road)' (in F minor) has I, III, V, VI and VII; 'The River' (in E minor) uses I, III, IV, VI, and VII. Among the six-chord songs, 'Cover Me' uses I, III, IV, V, VI, and VII in B minor (Bm D Em F# G A); the same chords in E minor feature in 'Spirit In The Night' but with the minor chord V (Bm). 'Because The Night' adds a rarer bII chord (C in B minor) to its I, III, V, VI and VII.

'Murder Incorporated' (in E minor) uses a four-chord turnaround of Em D G A (I VII III IV$^\wedge$) for both verse and chorus, but as it approaches the hook-line the rate of chord change gives each chord a bar instead of half a bar, thus stretching it out. The bridge brings in a minor chord V (Bm) but after the guitar solo a VI-V (C-B) change leads back to the verse. So chord V is present both as a major and a minor chord – making 'Murder Incorporated' a good example of a song that uses the songwriter's composite minor.

KEY CHANGES
'THE TIES THAT BIND', 'WHERE THE BANDS ARE', 'LONESOME DAY'

A song doesn't have to stay in one key. Changing key is a powerful way to create contrasts in your songs. The following discussion provides some basic information so you can consider using a key change yourself.

Why change key?

A key-change reduces monotony and takes the listener on a journey. It can refresh a section that has already been heard, usually more than once, by presenting it at a different pitch. Traditionally, it is the chorus that is most likely to move into a different key toward the end of a song. After the last verse or bridge or solo, the chorus is heard first in the home key and then on repetition is heard in a new key. Alternatively, the final chorus follows the last verse immediately in the new key, which is more startling. In pop tradition this type of key-change is either up one semitone or a tone.

If your song has a repeating section, key-changing enables it to be repeated with more interest. This is handy with turnarounds. Key-changing can contrast different parts of a song, as when the bridge is in a new key. If something in your lyric suggests a new perspective (literal or metaphorical – new love, new job, new town, new emotion) a key-change can make the listener feel it rather than the song just telling them it is so. If your new lover makes you feel like you've never felt before (to use a lyric cliché) why not say so (to the listener, not to her!) with a key-change?

How many keys are there?

There is a major key and a minor key on each of the 12 notes, giving 24 in total. However, three majors and three minors are written out enharmonically as both a sharp key and a flat key. These keys are B major (also Cb major), F# major (Gb major), C# major (Db major) and their relative minors G# minor (also Ab minor), D# minor (Eb minor), and A# minor (Bb minor). Songwriters who play guitar favour keys that permit open-string chords. In open position on the guitar these are F, C, G, D, A and E major. These are the shapes that will most frequently occur in your songs. Any other key may provoke the use of a capo to remove tiring barre chords. If a song starts in any major or minor key there are 23 other keys to which it could change.

Near keys and far keys

Some keys are related to the home key because they have notes and chords in common. Some are not related because they have few notes and chords in common.

A 'near' key is one that can be reached relatively easily from the home key. It requires a minimal number of new accidentals in the melody, and the change will not perturb the listener. Only one chord is required to reach an important chord in a near key. It is easy to return from this key to the home key.

A 'distant' key is one that can be reached only with some ingenuity from the home key. It requires considerable adjustment of accidentals in the melody; the change will sound unusual to the listener, even unsettling if not adequately prepared. Several chords are required to reach an important chord in the new key and likewise to get back again.

You can learn much about the effect of key-changes by listening to their effect in Springsteen's songs.

SPRINGSTEEN'S KEY CHANGES
THE TONE SHIFT

Songs that move up a tone include 'Mary's Place' which starts in F major, goes up a tone to G major at about the five minute mark and then drops back to F near the end. 'Hungry Heart' goes up a tone from C major to D major for an organ solo and then drops back for the last verse. 'Backstreets' changes key from G major up to A major with a dramatic chord change from Em to E to A at 2:42-45. It returns to G at 3:34 for the start of the guitar solo. 'I'm A Rocker' changes key from A major to B major on the bridge. 'The Ties That Bind' changes key up a tone from C major to D major for its last verse. Springsteen is fond of changing key for a solo in order to put that solo in a new context.

You can also change key down a tone. 'Counting On A Miracle' changes down a tone from A major to G major for its bridge. 'Racing In The Street' is in F major but the instrumental break takes it mournfully down to Eb major before returning to F major on the next verse.

The 'over-lap' three-chord trick

Here's a special application of the tone-up key change. 'The Ties That Bind' is a three-chord trick in C major which adds two more chords (D and A) to become a three-chord trick in D major when it changes key towards its last verse and chorus. I call this an 'over-lap' three-chord trick because if a song changes key up a tone (i.e. going from C major to D major) one chord will be common in the two three-chord tricks: compare C-F-G and D-G-A – the common 'over-lap' chord is G.

The same is available if you change key to the other near keys. (Common chords are in bold, the home key is C major, the near key is in brackets.)

C major = I		IV	V	Near key =	I	IV	V
C		**F**	G	(Bb major)	Bb	Eb	**F**
C		**F**	G	(F major)	**F**	Bb	C
C		F	**G**	(G major)	**G**	**C**	D
C		F	**G**	(D major)	D	**G**	A

Going to IV or V

You can also try other key-changes to such close destinations as the key represented by chord IV: 'Lonesome Day' transposes its IV-I chord movement from Bb major to Eb major for the guitar break. 'The Angel' changes from G major to C major at its bridge, around 2:16, gets established around 2:30 and returns to G major at 2:44. 'Code Of Silence' is in D major but transposes its main idea to G major for the sax solo. Sometimes a song can hover between keys, as in the case of 'Darlington County' which suggests G major and C major. 'I Wanna Be With You' is in D major but its prechorus is in A major (0:38-47) then it goes back to D major for the chorus. 'Fire' is in G major; its bridge ends with a traditional momentary key-change to D major.

It's possible to create the expectation of a key-change and then either not do it or do it later. 'Give The Girl A Kiss' is in G major. The bridge suggests it is changing to D major at the end via an A7 chord – but this doesn't happen until the coda, when it gets there by repeating the bridge and finally following through on the A7 to D major.

Exotic key-changes

For more exotic effects try wandering further afield among the keys. 'Linda Let Me Be The One' transposes its chorus sequence into E major for the sax solo and on the next verse returns to G major. 'Jungleland' changes key from C major to Eb major. Alternatively, you can change key from major to minor: 'Let's Be Friends' is in C major but its bridge is in D minor. 'Wages Of Sin' pits an E major verse against an ambiguous G major-ish chorus using the chords G, C and Em. 'Roulette' starts in D minor but the guitar solo suggests a change to A minor. 'The E Street Shuffle' is mostly in C major but ends with a guitar solo (at 3:06) and coda in Bb minor. The key change is emphasised by the pause and the sudden increase in tempo.

Multiple key-changes

A song can have more than one key-change. 'Where The Bands Are' is in D major, changes to E major for its sax solo and moves the same sequence into G major for eight bars of guitar solo. 'Waiting On A Sunny Day' changes key up a tone from C major to D major and then back, although for the sax solo at the end the song pushes its basic sequence of I-VI-IV-I-V into E major. 'Born To Run' changes key from E major to G major momentarily in the bridge on the words "scream" and "huddled". The guitar solo immediately after is in the key of F, a distant key from the home key of E major, but the distance is fitting for a tale of people on the run.

Always consider whether there is something in your lyric that could be illustrated with a key-change of some kind for that section.

Multiple key-changes play a big part in making 'Kitty's Back' and 'Candy's Room' two of Springsteen's greatest songs. 'Kitty's Back' has three keys. It begins with A minor, fluctuates to A major at 1:29, goes back to A minor at 1:42. The "Kitty's back in town" refrain at 4:55-5:20 is in F#m. The song goes back to A minor at 5:38, the key in which it finishes.

'Candy's Room' is in G major. The verse is in a mixolydian G: with the chords G Dm F C. The guitar solo is in B minor (I, VII, VI, Vm and IV^) which then jumps into C for the bridge's "she has fancy clothes" which is C to G followed by a Dm then F. The key contrasts are fully integrated in these songs; it isn't simply a matter of shoving the song up a tone on its last chorus as happens all too predictably on many hit songs.

Ambiguous key changes

Sometimes it isn't always clear which key the music is in. This can create a certain ambiguity, as is certainly felt in 'Night'. It seems to open in F major, but the verse is more centred on a Bb chord. The impression of Bb major as the home key is strengthened when Bruce sings "pretty" (at 0:30, 1:22) where we get Eb F Gm (IV-V-VI in Bb major). However, this finds its way back to the Fsus4-F change via Gm Cm C7 – the C7 indicates the change back into F major. No sooner has it done this than it transposes the rising chord idea into Eb major to get Ab Bb Cm (0:49, 1:40, 2:25). This in turn heads back to F major at 1:02. Just to further blur things, the bridge (1:59) throws in a bVII Eb chord on the word "inside". F mixolydian's chords are naturally suggestive of Bb major. But the song definitely ends in F major.

Technique summary

This second section has dealt with chords and chord progressions, and has shown you how to use the following songwriting techniques:

- the two-chord song;
- the I-VI and I-IV change;
- using a pedal note under a simple change;
- the three-chord trick;
- the over-lap three-chord trick;
- the three-chord trick without; chord V;
- displacing a chord;
- withholding a chord;
- substituting with an inversion;
- varying the rate of chord change;
- the four-chord song;
- the four-chord turnaround;
- the escalator effect;

- the five- and six-chord song;
- the mixolydian song;
- using chromatic chord changes;
- turning majors into minors;
- using a lowered degree chord;
- chromatic build-ups;
- chossing your final chord;
- writing a song in a minor key;
- using a key change;
- near and far keys;
- the tone-shift key change;
- the IV or V key-change;
- exotic, ambiguous and multiple key changes.

Even if you have been writing songs for some time there is plenty here for you to work into your music and try out in new songs. In Sections 1 and 2 we've covered many techniques deployed by songwriters as they piece together material. But the next challenge is getting that music played and recorded, and that means working with others. The next step is studio and stage.

SECTION 3
studio and stage

A songwriter who composes a song on his or her own can reproduce the song alone. But significant things happen to your song when it is given to a group of people – ie, a band – to play, in the studio or onstage. Sometimes this results in considerable differences between your demo performance and the finished recording. It's a bit like the difference between a pencil sketch and an oil painting. So what can be learned about this element of music-making from the recording and performance aspects of Springsteen's music?

If you're in a band, what kind of band? How many of you are there? It's funny how we often find ourselves in bands without necessarily having thought much about why we should have a particular line-up of instruments. Often, things fall together that way because those are the people available at the time. The band that starts as a five-piece prog-rock outfit ends as a rock trio because the keyboard player emigrates and the second guitarist is unreliable.

The quintessential rock band is guitar, bass, drums and a voice. This can mean three or four people, depending on whether the voice comes from someone who is solely a singer. The harmony bit of the music is generated by a mere 10 strings (4 on bass, 6 on guitar), so this is a minimal set-up. With it the aim is to make enough sound to a) get a full musical picture, b) make sure the harmony offsets the drums, c) keep the harmony going if the guitar takes a solo, and d) keep the voice supported. But some people need a bigger sound with more musical colour than this line-up can provide. This is the case with Bruce and the E Streeters.

The big band

As a songwriter Bruce Springsteen always had a cinematic quality. In describing his songs he has sometimes used cinematography terms – like panning in and out. It's no accident that his debut *Greetings From Asbury Park, New Jersey* (1973) was named after a town and a state, and *The Wild, The Innocent And The E Street Shuffle* sounds like a film title in itself. The songs are peopled with many characters; the sheer size of America has always been present in his writing. Such a musical vision required a big band to put it across. Enter The E Street Band, one of the best live acts to ever tread the boards.

Springsteen made his reputation as a knock-out 'must see' concert draw. The E Street Band are an essential part of his concert success. They are in many ways the quintessential American rock band because they represent the team ethic behind the national motto, *E pluribus unum* – 'Out of many, one'.

The E Street Band have been nothing less than a rock'n'roll orchestra. They took songs and arranged them as mini-epics of such intensity they were bound to get audiences rocking. Just imagine being in a band with two guitars (later four), two keyboards (organ and piano), drums, bass, backing vocals and sax (and recently violin from Soozie Tyrell). This is much bigger than the average four-piece rock band. In fact, you need to look into the soul/R&B field to find an equivalent. Now think of all that going through a P.A. That's a lot of musical resource but a pretty hefty sound to manage.

Playing in and leading a band like that takes discipline and musical suss. Otherwise, instruments get in the way of each other, occupying the same frequencies and the sound becomes muddy and incoherent. This is true whether the mix is a studio one or a live one. Players have to be disciplined with their individual parts, so that each contributes to the whole. The E Street Band's collective ability to harness this huge musical potential and create performances like 'Born To Run' (in emulation of Phil Spector's wall-of-sound), 'Thunder Road' or 'Rosalita' is unparalleled. It also means that if 'The Boss' wants to stop playing guitar and concentrate on singing for a while, or working the crowd, he's free to do so. In the most recent E Street Band there are three other guitars behind him.

To cite two examples, The E Street Band is never short of a soloist is one is required. If there's a guitar break, Springsteen, 'Miami' Steve Van Zandt or Nils Lofgren are equally adept at taking a lead break, and if a guitar solo is not what's needed Clarence Clemons can always provide a burst of sax. Secondly, the band arrangements make good use of the line-up's vocal potential in the way the different voices sing the phrase "41 shots" at the start of 'American Skin' and throughout 'If I Should Fall Behind' during the versions recorded for the *Live In New York City* album.

Interviewed in *Mojo* in 1995, shortly after he had got the band back together to record some new songs for the *Greatest Hits* album, Springsteen commented, "I realised there was a certain way that I write when I'm writing for those guys to play, a little broader in some sense than the area I was working in."

Arrangements

Arranging is a musical art in itself. It means knowing how to use the instrumentation available to frame your songs in the best way. The more players in your band, the more choices. In a power trio of guitar, bass and drums the choices are limited. In the current E Street Band, with its nine or ten players, the choices are enormous – they have hardly scratched the surface.

There has always been the option of taking the studio version and extending it by making different instruments more of a feature with solos or jamming sections. Van Zandt said, "We would always change the arrangement of the songs live. We could stretch them out and stuff … we'd take them somewhere else, make the live show just a trip." As a guitarist Van Zandt is aware of the problematic balance between guitars and keyboards in a rock band: "It's always a little tricky in the E Street situation, because we have two keyboards and that takes up a lot of space. We were very careful on *The River* and *Born In The USA*. We were consciously trying to get the balance a little more in favour of the guitars; we weren't using B-3 organs as much as smaller, Farfisa-type things. The frequency range was quite a bit smaller. It's a bit tricky, and you have to consciously work at that."

A similar awareness is evident in Springsteen's description to *Uncut* in 2002 of how he felt the band needed to find a new sonic shape for the recording of *The Rising* album: "The guitars were brought way up front, the keyboards were put in a different spot, things sounded a little different. We used a variety of different tape loops, and we had a lot of different sounds going on – everything to sort of not get to the normal thing that we'd done in the past. The essential thing was to get the band to feel sonically fresh."

Instrumentation

Springsteen's *rock* music (not all of what he does is rock) is traditional, in so far as it harks back to 1950s rock'n'roll, Elvis, Chuck Berry, Orbison, Phil Spector, 1960s R&B and British Invasion bands for its main points of reference. Such music is traditionally played with guitars, bass and drums, secondarily piano (think Jerry Lee Lewis and Little Richard). With The E Street Band and multi-track recording, he has always had many options in terms of additional instruments. So let's consider some specific examples of instrumentation and what these extra instrumental colours brought to a track.

The most famous 'extra' instrument in Springsteen's music is on the cover of *Born To Run*: Clarence Clemons's saxophone. Sax often provides the point of release in a Springsteen song that a guitar solo would provide in other bands. It does so in 'She's The One' and many other numbers. Sometimes the sax doubles or harmonises with a lead guitar line, as in 'Rosalita'. However, there's more to it than that. The sax also interacts with the rhythm guitar parts on tunes like 'Seaside Bar Song' and 'Born To Run' where multi-tracked it drones fifths. This effect strengthens the bottom end and adds grit to the lower guitar parts. Other brass parts worth listening to include muted trumpet on 'With Every Wish' and 'Meeting Across The River' (giving a jazz feel), and the comical brass-band tuba on 'Wild Billy's Circus Story'.

Apart from sax, the other extra (and distinctly un-rock'n'roll) instrument that became a classic part of the Springsteen sound is the glockenspiel. He probably got this from early 1960s Phil Spector productions. The 'glock' (as it is nicknamed) gives a glittery chime to many tracks, for example on 'Born To Run' and 'Loose Ends' (which also seems to have sleigh bells on it toward the end), often doubling at a higher pitch musical figures played on piano. It has become something of an in-joke. In connection with its use on *The Rising*, Springsteen told *Uncut* in 2002, "Brendan O'Brien [the producer] played it on 'Into The Fire' and 'Waitin' On A Sunny Day'. He was going, 'I'm doing a Springsteen record! Damn right I'm gonna play the glockenspiel!'"

Other instrumental colours to listen for include the congas just before the sax solo on 'Spirit In The Night', the accordion on the chorus of '4th of July, Asbury Park (Sandy)', the dual mandolins in 'Wild Billy's Circus Story', the use of harmonica on *The Ghost Of Tom Joad* to enhance the camp-fire melancholy of the folk style, and the Doors-like Gothic organ touches and swells on 'Lost In The Flood', especially on the coda. Springsteen has not made great use of strings on his records, but they do play a part in 'Jungleland' and at the back of the mix on the last verse of 'Born To Run'. On *The Rising* the strings come upfront. There's what sounds like a string quartet on the bridge of 'Counting On A Miracle' and cello on 'My City Of Ruins' in a manner that recalls the cello on the end of 'The Angel'.

Instruments can also be used to illustrate a specific point in a lyric. In 'Jungleland' the line "from the churches to the jails" is matched by the entry of an organ, an instrument associated with churches. On other occasions what might be needed is silence, as in 'Lost In The Flood' where the lyric says "everything stops" and shortly after the music does stop for the phrase "five quick shots".

Dynamics

All great rock bands understand the importance of dynamics, of playing loud against playing soft, and how dynamics can make your song twice as exciting onstage in front of an audience. If you have four guitars and two keyboards do you want them playing all at once, all of the time? Certainly not. Whether live or on disc, you don't want your audience to get tired of hearing the same sound, nor do you want to expend all that power flat out all the time. It's a matter of treating the instruments as a palette of colours. Springsteen's music is full of dynamic contrast. There are examplesof this all over the *Live 1975-85* set.

He also incorporates dynamics into the studio cuts. Listen for the way 'Into The Fire' erupts into its second verse, or to the violent contrast between the verse and the chorus in 'Darkness On The Edge Of Town', or to how the drums are held back in 'The Rising'. The intro of 'I Wanna Be With You' has guitar chords and then an explosion of drums at 1:16, delayed until the first verse and chorus are over, just after Bruce's "huh!". 'Lost In The Flood' is piano and vocal until 2:00 when bass and drums enter to push the song forward. Drums, bass and sax all enter to lift the first chorus of '4th of July, Asbury Park (Sandy)'. By contrast there are songs whose arrangement is stripped back initially to rhythm section and voice. '57 Channels (And Nothing On)' is drums and bass with voice only for the first verse. 'Over The Rise' is vocal, bass and cymbal for the first verse – so there are no chords until verse 2 when there's a quiet keyboard part. Likewise the first verse of 'When The Lights Go Out' has drum, bass, no chords, and the keyboard fills things out for verse 2.

Let's look in more detail at the dynamic curve of a single song. This will give you an idea of how you can make your songs more effective when you perform them. 'Racing In The Streets' has a gentle ebb and flow across its 6:50 duration and no big finish to release the tension. Here are the song's sections with a note of instruments entering or leaving the mix. The mix never stays the same for very long, and the piano sometimes sounds as though it is coming from a single direction (mono) and at other times coming from both sides (stereo).

'Racing In The Streets'

Intro	solo piano mono	Verse 3		piano + vocal only
Verse 1	piano in stereo + vocal in		3:25	backing vocal in
Chorus 1			4:20	thicker backing vocals
Verse 2	wood-block, hi-hat in		4:34	piano goes back to mono
	1:54	bass guitar, organ in		4:48	piano stereo
Chorus 2	snare drum, guitar in			solo piano in stereo
Link		Coda	5:15	wood-block, hi-hat, organ, piano
			5:37	bass guitar in + tambourine
			6:00	guitar in stereo playing arpeggio
			6:23	second guitar in stereo

The quiet last verse

It is a mannerism in Springsteen's songwriting to take the volume down for the last verse. This is a sensible, if over-used, technique for rock songs because the idea is to give your audience a break from the onslaught after they've had two verse, two choruses and a solo or a bridge. You want the last choruses to have maximum impact, so the music is pulled back quieter and with sparser instrumentation to contrast with the rousing full-on attack of the last chorus.

In many Springsteen songs this works very well. 'Growin' Up' has a last verse which is piano and vocal only; 'The Price You Pay' and 'Prove It All Night' also strip everything back on their last verse. 'Something In The Night' cuts down to a voice and a drum-beat; we add the harmony for ourselves in our mind because we've already heard several verses and know what the chords are. 'Better Days' drops back after the solo; 'My Beautiful Reward' pulls out the drums for the last verse and the chorus that follows. 'Part Man Part Monkey' thins out the drums and bass leaving just cymbals, and organ. This is still done on the most recent studio album *The Rising*. 'Mary's Place' takes the volume down toward the end before bringing it back up, as does 'The Rising', and 'You're Missing' with its string pizzicato.

Build-ups

One songwriting technique Springsteen has always deployed effectively is the build-up. This is a section where tension and anticipation are generated by having the music indicate that there is about to be a transition. This can be done in a number of ways:

- The volume might go from soft to loud;
- The chord progression might stay on a single chord (sus4 chords are good for this because they demand resolution);
- There might be a forceful ascending or descending progression which is obviously heading toward something – like the return of the riff or the chorus.

In concert a band can really wind an audience up with these, even teasing the crowd by lengthening such a passage beyond the original recorded version with which they are familiar. Here are some examples from Springsteen.

The prechorus of 'My Love Will Not Let You Down' has five bars of chord IV before hitting the chorus. Listen to the six bars of two chords building up in 'The Fever' from 4:42. The middle-eight of 'Working On The Highway' lasts 11 bars (an example of the '8+1' formula), the last four bars of which are a build-up on chord V (a G). The build-up doesn't even need to land where it might be expected to go. In 'Janey Don't You Lose Heart' at end of the chorus from 2:50-56 the music builds on chord V suggesting it will land on chord I. Instead it goes to another chorus, the chorus in this song starting on chord IV.

Your song could even have more than one build-up, or more than one version of the same build-up. The early song 'For You' has several crescendoes that lead to a chorus, each of which get longer. The first is six bars, the second is eight bars, and the third in the last verse is 16 bars. 'Backstreets' has no less than three, not counting the intro. At 4:40 the music is stripped back to piano and a Motownesque bass-line. As Bruce sings "hiding on the backstreets" gradually more instruments enter. This build-up continues to 5:34 where there is a first climax. There's another at 5:54-6:00, and a third at 6:13 where the drums drop to a brief half-time feel before the track ends at 6:28.

Chromatic chord sequences – where the chords move in semitone steps – make good build-ups because they inevitably involve out-of-key (and therefore tense) chords. There's a short one in 'Rosalita'. 'Born To Run' has the Mother of All Build-Ups after the guitar solo when the band plays an ascending and descending sequence which uses all 12 major chords, eventually landing on a sustained chord V held for four bars ended by the most famous 1...2...3...4... count in rock. And that isn't all, because the last chorus of 'Born To Run' turns itself into a build-up by including the singing of the lyric hook-line several times before it finally lands on the riff and chord I (E).

Accented chords

Both dynamics generally and build-ups specifically can use accented chords. One of the most common missed opportunities in singer-songwriter material is the 'passive' presentation of a chord progression. What I mean by 'passive' is simply strumming the chords in a fairly even way, rhythm and volume-wise, all on a level. This is functional but not always as interesting as it could be, especially if the song is meant to excite people. To stop yourself doing this remember this phrase: what is so interesting about a strummed guitar? Now make it interesting.

So, before demoing a song, when the melody, progression and structure are sorted out, take another look and ask yourself: can I accent some of these changes so that they jump out?

Springsteen and the E Street Band are very good at this. All you have to think of is the sheer punch of the intro Asus2 chord on 'The Ties That Bind', the way the first chords of 'Prove It All Night' are whacked out sledgehammer style, the accented chords of the coda of 'Lost In The Flood' and toward the end of the sax solo in 'Loose Ends'. Accented chords are all over 'Backstreets' (as at 4:35) and part of the power of the chorus to 'Streets Of Fire'.

Accented chords don't only mean a rock thump-thump. Listen for how the accented chords at 4:34-37 in 'Kitty's Back' ("get ready, get tight, get down") make Springsteen sound rakish as a funk Sinatra. In 'The Fever' (at 5:19) they prevent the constant swing of what is a seven minute track getting monotonous. The louder accented chords which interrupt at 6:30 contrast with the dynamic which is generally quiet. You can use them to emphasise a change of section – consider the B-E chords at 2:08 in 'Born To Run' that mark the end of the sax solo. One of the best examples, because of its inventiveness, happens in 'She's The One' using E and A. It starts at 3:35-56 and the band play different accents each time.

Varying the beat

Springsteen's musical conservatism has meant that he has tended to stick to 4/4, like many rock acts. Occasionally, in songs like the jazzy 'The Fever', 'Valentine's Day' and 'Lion's Den' the music swings, implying a possible 12/8 signature (though this is still four beats in a bar). But you don't have to change time signature to vary the pulse of your music. Springsteen's earlier music has many fine examples of changing the tempo, pulling the music up or pushing it faster, sometimes in the same song. It is a pity that this device has disappeared from his music.

'Thunder Road' doesn't establish its true tempo until the vocal enters. Its piano plus harmonica intro starts the song slower and then gradually accelerates to that memorable first image of the screen door slamming. The opening guitar solo of 'Kitty's Back' is slower than the main body of the song. 'Lost In The Flood' pulls back its tempo as it reduces down to voice, piano and organ at 2:58. When the drums enter a few beats later you can hear that it's slower than it had been. 'Spirit In The Night' slows right down for its last verse at 3:24 with voice and piano only, recovering the original tempo at 4:04. 'Does This Bus Stop At 82nd St?' pulls up at the phrase "uptown in Harlem" for the segue into 'Lost In The Flood'. 'The E Street Shuffle' has a false ending at 3:36, which then turns into a faster coda with sax riffing over a frenetic funk work-out until the fade at 4:24. 'New York City Serenade' begins with a free-time piano intro with no discernible regular pulse until the tempo is established when it first plays the main chord progression for most of the song. 'Jungleland' has a number of tempi – it starts off slow and then doubles up.

Where Springsteen really makes this varying of the beat tell is in his early acoustic songs – one reason why there is a case for them being musically superior to later material like the *Nebraska* and *The Ghost of Tom Joad* sets. In 'Mary Queen Of Arkansas' the song is made dramatic by its fluctuating tempo. Springsteen slows down or speeds up according to what he's singing. We feel his urgency, doubt and reluctance through the changing speed of the music. For example, 3:06-20 has a rapidly accelerating passage and gets louder. He does the same thing toward the end at 4:50-5:01, heading toward the word "contacts". The same technique enlivens another acoustic song 'Wild Billy's Circus Story', with its raked chords, pulling up at 2:50 and again at 3:02 and 3:18, before picking up the original tempo. In a time when click-tracks and beatboxes have straitjacketed tempo, such a technique now seems in retrospect daring and expressive.

Using keyboards

Keyboards make a huge background contribution to The E Street Band's sound. David Sancious (on the first two albums), Roy Bittan and Danny Frederici are responsible for many magic moments on Bruce Springsteen songs. The keyboards are often used to add a melodic motif where in another band there might be a guitar riff. In 'Valentine's Day' there's a rising three-note motif and around the 4:30 mark the keyboards get denser with a descending arpeggio figure to the fade. Organ and piano play a similar melodic motif in unison on the coda of 'Loose Ends'. 'Secret Garden' has a three-note keyboard motif repeated over the chord changes. It was keyboards that played the hook/riff in 'Born In The USA'. Other examples include the single-note 'telegraph' figure at the start of 'I Wanna Be With You' coupled with sustained organ chords – the piano note doesn't change over the changing chords; the motif going down the scale in 'Janey Don't You Lost Heart' on the chorus and continuing through the sax solo; and the Farfisa-type high organ solo at the end of 'Two Faces'. 'Incident on 57th Street' actually has two pianos, one either side of the mix.

Even outside the context of The E Street Band, Springsteen's recordings can be checked out for some useful tips on using keyboards. Many songs Springsteen recorded on his own or with session players deploy what are known as keyboard 'pads'. These involve selecting a keyboard sound with a long sustain, not much in the way of high frequencies, and a certain soft, thick quality. The idea is to fill in the back of the mix with this sound, rather as though you were covering a canvas with a single muted dark colour against which other things will stand out in relief even if they themselves are not assertive, spikey or loud figures. To cast this in a metaphor that suits Springsteen's music, imagine a cream-painted car against a stormy purple horizon – the car stands out all the more.

You certainly don't have to be a keyboard virtuoso to play such 'pads' in a mix. Plenty of sustain means that even if you're not that quick making a chord change on the keys the notes are still hanging while your fingers move to the next chord. You don't need to hold down many notes at a time, either. A simple major or minor chord is only three notes, so you can play a triad with one hand on the keyboard. You might need only two notes – in which case play fifths and let the guitar part or the vocal melody signal whether a chord is major or minor by including the note that you have omitted from the keyboard part.

This muted keyboard pad idea is something Springsteen used to generate atmosphere on albums like *Tunnel Of Love* and *The Ghost Of Tom Joad*. It goes well with guitar because the guitar has the brighter frequencies, and especially with the rustling, dry tone of finger-picked notes, which don't sustain for very long.

'Cautious Man' makes good use of muted keyboard to sketch the haunted predicament of a character called Bill Horton. 'I'm On Fire' has the same idea, the synth playing an unresolved 9th (the note F#) over the link C#m-E change. In 'Brothers Under The Bridge' the pad is brought in on the second verse. The keyboards on 'Sad Eyes' produce one of the great moments in all of Springsteen's music, in the quiet last verse on the phrase "blue, blue ribbon" (2:18-33) where all the other instruments except the keyboard synth die away, leaving a snatch of mysterious chords brooding like Fate itself.

If you write songs on guitar you should consider getting familiar enough with a keyboard to be able to add rudimentary touches to your demos. It only takes a couple of notes to make a difference. You could even try writing on it. That iconic image on the cover of *Born To Run* of Bruce with his Fender guitar shouldn't make us forget that he has written many songs on piano. In *Songs* he said of his third album, "The orchestral sound of *Born To Run* came from most of the songs being written on the piano. It was on the keyboard that I could find the arrangements needed to accompany the stories I was writing."

Backing vocals

Your songs can be enhanced by the use of backing vocals and vocal harmonies.

Occasionally Springsteen has created a similar effect to the keyboard 'pad' with a backing vocal that sustains a note behind the lead vocal. This background voice usually has plenty of reverb in the mix to push it into the distance so it doesn't distract from the main voice. You can hear this in 'Racing In The Streets', in the second verse of 'Loose Ends' where Bruce sings D against the G-Em chord change, and in 'The Promised Land' where there is a held D backing note on the last verse over a G-Em-C change. The harmonic value of this D changes as the chords change. It is a 5th of G (and therefore part of the simple triad of G: G B D), a 7th of Em (part of E G B D), and a 9th against the C chord (C E G D) – so the note becomes progressively more tense.

Backing vocals are often thought of as a harmony device, and its true that there is some wonderful harmonizing in places like the choruses of '4th Of July (Sandy)' and

'Incident On 57th Street'. The female voices on *The Rising* underscore the gospel feel of some of the songs. In early songs like 'Thundercrack' and 'Kitty's Back' there are outbursts of male voices in chants or mock-squabbles emphasising the idea of the band as a gang. Bruce occasionally harmonises with himself in conventional thirds, the main interval used for vocal harmony, (you can hear him do so in 'Two Hearts') but occasionally he has made effective use of the backing vocal as an answering second voice, as on 'Atlantic City', and on the chorus of 'One Step Up', where Patti Scialfa replies each time to his enunciation of the title.

Implied chords

One important arrangement technique that gets easier as you have more players in your band is the implied chord. The implied chord is a less emphatic way to harmonise a song than the standard technique of strumming chords. There are two basic approaches to this:

First, strip back the playing so that the chords of a given song section – like a verse or chorus – are only faintly sketched in. The simplest way to do this is to have no guitars or keyboards playing full chords, only one-note-at-a-time melodic figures, with the bass playing root notes. That way you can present a verse and/or chorus without yet stating the chords, which can then be brought in on the second verse with a certain drama. 'Ain't Got You' has a first verse, in Bo Diddley rhythm, sung without instruments; we have to imagine what the chords will be.

Second, give the chords a new colour by having a single bass note under them (a 'pedal' note) or altered root notes. In both instances the bass note has an authority that causes the listener's ear to reinterpret the chords above it; the bass note over-rules the identity of the chords. The chord of Bm7 consists of the notes B D F# A. Put a B in the bass underneath a D chord of D F# A and that's what you get: an implied Bm7. Put a G under a D chord and you get an implied Gmajor9 without a third: Gmajor9 is G B D F# A.

Implied chords are excellent for playing variations on sequences that have already happened in a song. Imagine a tune in which the Dsus4-D-Dsus2-D change has been played as a link or part of a verse. Instead of repeating it for the coda a new dimension is given by making the bass play different notes.

Here's a Springsteen example: 'Take 'Em As They Come' implies other chords by having the bass hold first G and then B under the D-Dsus4-D-Dsus2 riff. The result is an implied harmony that exists because of the aggregate of instruments, not because of one instrument alone. The first verse of 'Working On The Highway' has an implied chord sequence of I-IV-V-VI only made explicit on the second verse.

Pedal notes

One way to do this is to use a pedal note (first mentioned in Section 2). The verse of 'Lion's Den' puts a IV-I chord change over a C pedal (the key note) for 7 bars. In 'I Wanna Be With You' the bass puts a D pedal note under the first chords (I, IV and V, three bars). The opening bars of 'Born To Run' put the I-IV-V change over a key-note (tonic) pedal of E, and does same thing after the first hook line. 'Tenth Avenue Freeze-Out' has an implied chord change in that the F-Dm (I-VI) change is played on piano and bass but not followed by the guitar which only sounds the I. 'Backstreets' starts its initial guitar riff and verse with I-VI in G, after a piano intro where the I-VI is held over a throbbing tonic pedal G. Pedal notes have the effect of suspending a chord sequence, so that when the bass root notes start the sequence suddenly sounds grounded and stronger.

Studio and stage checklist

In this section we have looked at a variety of issues and ideas that bear on the process of getting your songs across to people. We can summarise this material in the form of a checklist of questions. In the context of your songs:

- Do you have the right band line-up?
- Do you have the instruments you need for your type of music?
- Do you need acoustic and electric guitar?
- Do you need keyboards?
- Do you need extra percussion in addition to a drum-kit?
- Would your music get by without a drum-kit?
- Do you need another voice singing and / or backing vocals?
- Do you want a less common feature instrument to take solos?
- How much volume does your music need to sound at its best?
- Are your songs effective played live?
- Do they need extended sections for improvising?
- Do you enough variety of solos?
- Are your songs making good use of dynamics?
- Are your songs creating excitement with build-ups?
- Are you getting power from accented chords?
- Could your live set benefit from a song in a time other than 4/4?
- Do your songs make use of slowing up or accelerating?

guitar techniques

This section focuses on the role of the guitar in Springsteen's music. It is an important area and one from which guitarists who aspire to write their own material can learn a crucial lesson. For it was only when Springsteen decided that he was a songwriter who happened to play guitar, rather than a guitarist first and foremost, that he found his musical direction. Guitarists who write songs are prone to confuse guitar-playing with songwriting. They make up riffs and sequences that are fun to play on the instrument – but such things do not necessarily make a song.

Remember: you haven't really got a song until you have a melody and a lyric.

In 'Thunder Road' Springsteen looked back on his youth and sang, "Well, I got this guitar and I learned how to make it talk." But having achieved fretboard prowess, he decided it wasn't enough. He told *Guitar World* in 1995, "I was always the guitar player in the band. But I reached a point in the early Seventies where I said, 'There are so many good guitarists, but there are not a lot of people who have their own songwriting voice.' And I finally focused on that … Ultimately, my guitar playing came to be about fitting in with the ensemble. Then Clarence came along with his saxophone. He's sort of a force of nature, so if I wanted to hear a solo, I let him do it … At some point I sort of opted out of the jam thing and got more into the solo being in service of the song." In 1977 he pointed out that "there's a million guitar players out there all whacking away … one big drone. So I decided I wasn't going to play unless I had to."

Songwriter first, guitarist second

This shift in perspective from guitar-centred rock to song-centred rock has also been commented on by 'Miami' Steve Van Zandt: "By '72, pretty much everything had shifted to the songs. By '72, pretty much everything that could be done with a guitar had been done, with the exception of Eddie Van Halen, who had yet to come. What were you gonna do that Clapton, Beck, Page and Hendrix hadn't done? … The emphasis had to shift to songs. However good a guitar player you were at that point, you had now to work within the context of a song: our guitar playing was gonna come in handy and be useful, but not so much to just go off on long solos to impress somebody anymore." Once this shift was made in Springsteen's music it was permanent. Van Zandt: "I've gotta say, the focus has never varied much from the songwriting being the priority. There are moments in *Darkness* … but the guitars were never a priority."

Playing guitar with keyboards

This question of emphasis has also spilled over into how the other guitarists approach their craft with The E Street Band. Not only are guitars not the priority, they don't have to cover so much harmonic space with two keyboard players present. Nils Lofgren in *Guitar World*: "It's such a big sound, with so much going on, I found myself almost not playing anything. It was like, 'I can play here, but why?' I looked for real, little simple rhythmic parts that would fit in. That's what I love about The E Street Band – there's such a big sound that I don't have to be playing all the time. I can craft some simple parts that are subtle but really serve the sound." In *Guitarist* he said, "If Bruce is playing his Tele, and Steve picks up his Strat, you really don't need another one, so on some electric songs I've been playing rhythm on Fender Jazzmasters." Lofgren further differentiates his sound from the other guitars by putting heavy gauge strings on his instrument.

Springsteen is a fine and characterful lead guitarist when he wants to be, and in a moment we'll look at some of the defining traits of his solos. Despite the fact that the guitar is a team player in his music there are memorable arrangement details to note. Often what might have been a guitar riff in another band is turned into a keyboard motif, as in 'Born In The USA', 'Lonesome Day' and 'Land Of Hope And Dreams'. Acoustic guitars are used to double the electrics on the main riff of 'She's The One', adding sparkle even though later they get drowned out. There's a great use of wah-wah on the right side of the mix in the sus2 bridge in 'Born To Run', echo guitar on the right side of 'Incident On 57th Street', and flanging on 'Brilliant Disguise'. And don't forget the drumming on the body of the acoustic guitar in 'Mary Queen Of Arkansas' to make the chords sound without actually hitting the strings.

BRUCE'S SOLOS

Although Springsteen is mainly thought of as a songwriter, he's a mean electric guitarist. Before signing with Columbia, he was a long-haired lead guitarist playing hard rock in bands like Steel Mill, emulating late 1960s guitar heroes. Springsteen found his own musical identity only when he abandoned the guitar hero role, took up his love of pre-Hendrix rock and soul/R&B, stole a leaf from the example of Dylan and Van Morrison, and emphasised words and songs. In 1975, Springsteen was startling because he didn't have long hair!

This wasn't a cynical career-move. Springsteen genuinely preferred songs. "When the guitar solos went on too long at the end of the 1960s, I lost interest," he once said. Van Zandt told *Guitar World*, "I hear his sound as a soup of all the best stuff we grew up with – a real heavy combination of the British Invasion, Jeff Beck, Jimmy Page, Clapton, plus that two- or three-note thing that Townshend and Keith Richards did. Add Motown and Jimi Hendrix and that's the soup our guitar styles came out of." But on the break-through record *Born To Run*, Springsteen tailored his guitar style to evoke an era before the blues boom when guitar riffs twanged on the lower, bass strings. As he admitted in 1987, "I wanted my guitar to sound like Duane Eddy."

On the coda of 'Thunder Road' there's a guitar solo of sorts. But it sure ain't Hendrix or Clapton. It's a melody played low, in sync with the sax. In short, it's pure Duane Eddy, the 1950s guitarist who had instrumental hits like 'Rebel Rouser' and 'Peter Gunn'. This type of break happens frequently in Springsteen songs, at least as much as the screaming stuff. Eddy's influence is palpable on 'Darkness on the Edge of Town', 'Man's Job', 'Tougher Than The Rest', 'Out On The Streets', 'The Wish', and on the riff to 'Backstreets'. The intro of 'Pink Cadillac' recalls a track like 'Peter Gunn'. This idea of the guitar playing a melody, rather than blues bends or scale-based widdling, is in a tradition that goes back to Eddy through Hank Marvin and sessioneer Vick Flick (who recorded the James Bond theme in Eddy's style).

A number of aspects to Springsteen's lead can be isolated. Each contributes to the character of his solos. The more of them combine at once the more the solo seems Springsteenesque.

Tone

In contrast to his earlier Les Paul humbucker days, Springsteen has favoured a wiry overdriven single-coil Fender tone, which he gets from his Esquire with an extra Telecaster pickup, and 1954, 1958 and 1963 Teles. This gives a treble boost to the ferocity of breaks like that in 'Trouble River'. In recent years he has featured a saturated distortion in which notes become fuzzy, as on the live 'American Skin (41 Shots)' and 'The Rising'. This fuzzy tone gives the notes considerable sustain. It also encourages fewer notes to let the tone come through – which it wouldn't if you were belting around the neck playing scales.

Working a few notes

Both the last two solos illustrate another aspect of his lead approach – which is to 'worry' away at a handful of notes in one or two positions. This gives the guitar-work on tracks like 'Adam Raised A Cain' and 'Streets Of Fire' a quality reminiscent of Neil Young. Some of his wiry lead sounds like Albert King.

At least two of Bruce's Telecasters are fitted with a 'tremolo' arm so that he can bring tremolo – or, more accurately, vibrato – to bear on any lead phrases. Occasionally he plays the type of traditional 'repeat licks' that most rock guitarists are familiar with, as at the end of the *Live in Barcelona* 'Prove It All Night'.

Rapid 'mandolin' strum

To add drama to his solos, Springsteen sometimes comes in rapidly picking a single note over and over, as though playing a mandolin. You can hear this on 'Adam Raised A Cain' and at the start of 'Cover Me'.

Pinch harmonics

Springsteen's solos have a rough texture to them. He emphasises the physicality of playing, so the listener is often aware of fingers fretting the strings so hard they go sharp, and the pick scraping the strings. This sometimes leads to pinch harmonics, as on 'Cover Me'.

Playing two notes at a time

Springsteen thickens his lead by using double-stops – playing two notes at a time. These include traditional sixths like the coda of 'Better Days'. In songs such as 'Restless Night', 'My Love Will Not Let You Down', 'American Skin (41 Shots)', and 'Man's Job', he selects pairs of notes that blend with the underlying chord. Songs like 'Cadillac Ranch' and 'Real World' use the traditional double-stops of Chuck Berry. As a fine example of harnessing lead guitar to the song, listen to the harmonizing lines that decorate the intro and verses of '4th of July, Asbury Park (Sandy)'.

Playing against an open string

One specific instance of playing two notes at a time in a lead break results when a fretted note is combined with an open string. In 'Worlds Apart' the solo pits a fretted E against an open E string. In 'Human Touch' and 'I Wish I Were Blind' the guitar solos work off the open G string by fretting the 2nd string. Use this to get a fuller sound.

Wide vibrato, wide bends

A lead guitarist's approach to bends and vibrato is one of his fingerprints. Springsteen's early solos are marked by a wide, slow vibrato and a willingness to push a bend a long way, including being careless of exact pitch. There are fine examples in 'Candy's Room', 'Kitty's Back', 'Roulette', 'Restless Night', and 'Incident on 57th Street'. Listen when the drums come in for a brief but typical Springsteen solo on the left using that wiry tone, lots of pronounced bends and pick attack on the strings.

Choice of notes

There's nothing unusual about Springsteen's choice of notes, though he avoids obvious pentatonic patterns. 'Adam Raised A Cain' is unusual in this regard but that is because it has such a strong, swampy blues character; the same is true of 'Missing'. The guitar solo in 'Part Man Part Monkey' has some C Dorian phrases over the minor sequence (C D Eb F G A Bb) and plenty of Bruce's steely phrasing. Perhaps his most adventurous moment (was it planned or a happy accident?) comes in 'My Love Will Not Let You Down', where the solo uses the eye-wateringly off-key note F# over the C major chords (in C the fourth note of the scale should be F not F#). The solos on 'One Step Up' and 'Roulette' show that ferocity is sometimes tempered by a melodic sense.

Phrasing

Springsteen's solos are often clearly phrased, as on 'Streets of Fire' and 'Cross My Heart', which has disciplined simple phrases over the chord changes. 'Further On (Up The Road)' uses part of the vocal melody in the solo – an old jazz trick.

If I had to pick two stand-out tracks for guitar lead they would be 'Kitty's Back' and 'Candy's Room'. The former is cleanly phrased, and lasts almost a minute. Its solo at 2:47-3:10 pits two guitars against each other left and right and includes matched harmonised bends, and there's a repeat lick at around 3:30. 'Candy's Room' opens with a single phrase played four times against four different chords before moving into some wild bending.

BRUCE'S CHORD SHAPES

As was described in Section 2, Springsteen writes his songs with a conservative range of chords. He makes comparatively little use of extended chords. There are a small number of types, in terms of sevenths and add9s, which contribute to the guitar-work on his recordings.

These chords are given later as chord-boxes at the pitches they occur most often in his songs.

The minor 7th

Minor 7th chords are heard on the early soul/funk influenced songs from the first three albums. The minor 7th adds to a simple minor chord the note a tone below the root. In a major key the three minor chords II, III and VI all take this form if they are turned from straight minors into 7ths. In C major this gives Dm7, Em7 and Am7. These chords are often easy to hold down. Their effect is to dilute the sadness of the minor chord with a dash of hope. This is because the minor 7th can be considered a fusion of a minor chord (C Eb G) with the major chord three semitones higher (Eb G Bb).

The main function of the minor 7th in Springsteen's songs is make a progression sound mildly jazzy or funky. 'The Fever' has extensive Am7, Bm7, and Em7 chords, 'Kitty's Back' has a slow Am7-Em7 groove in some parts, 'The E Street Shuffle' has a Bbm7-Ebm7 end sequence, and they also feature (sometimes pitched high on the neck) in the chorus of 'Spirit In The Night', in 'Tenth Avenue Freeze-Out', and throughout 'Blinded By The Light'. 'She's The One' also has high-pitched straight minors in its middle-eight.

Minor 7th 12-bar verse in B minor

I				Vm				IV				Vm		
Bm7	/	/	/	F#m7	/	/	/	Em7	/	/	/	/	F#m7	/

IV		VII		III		Vm		I				VII	IV	Vm	
Em7	/	A	/	D	/	F#m7		Bm7	/	/		A	Em7	/	F#m7	/

The suspended 2nd

Springsteen songs often feature the suspended 2nd chord. The suspended 2nd is neither major nor minor. The 3rd degree of the scale has been replaced ('suspended') by the 2nd of the scale. The 'sus2' is mildy dark, hollow, mysterious, tense but resigned. It combines well with the suspended fourth in 'indie'/'jangle' rock and often substitutes for A, Am, Dm and D because Asus2 and Dsus2 are easy shapes. If the 2nd is placed above the 5th (C G D), a '5add9' results. The 5add9 has a hard, stark power. In loud rock numbers the sus2 adds toughness to the sound, and in softer songs it is their hollow mysteriousness which is important.

All three chords of the three-chord trick (I, IV and V) can be turned into sus2 chords, and these sus2s can be used in addition to them in a song as variations of the harmony. So, as with inversions, a song that has A, Asus2, D, Dsus2, E and Esus2 is still really a three-chord trick.

In Springsteen's songs there are examples of I, IV and V being turned into sus2s. 'Walk Like A Man', 'The Promise', 'Racing In The Streets' and 'No Surrender' are all in F major and all use Bbsus2 (chord IV). 'Night' is the same – Csus2 (chord V) is the first chord you hear, played with a machine-gun strum. 'Jackson Cage' has Asus2 (IV) in the key of E and 'None But The Brave' has Asus2 in E in the verse and chorus; 'She's The One' (also in E) has Asus2 in the verse (on the word "soft" in verse 1). 'Prove It All Night' has a Dsus2 (chord IV in the key of A), the first chord in the chorus; 'New York City Serenade' (also in A) has a Dsus2 in its verse. It is also not uncommon to find both chord I and IV turned into sus2s, as happens in 'Out On The Streets' (Asus2 and Dsus2) or I and V, as occurs in 'The Ties That Bind' (Fsus2 and Csus2), or individually as V in 'Where The Bands Are' and 'I Wanna Be With You' (Asus2 in key of D), or I in the intro of 'Rendezvous' (Fsus2).

Sus2 verse idea in A

I				IV		I		I		V	
A	/	/	/	D	/	Dsus2	D	A	/	/	/

continued:

Asus2	/	E	/

IV				IV		I		V			
Dsus2	/	/	D	Dsus2	/	/	D	Asus2	/	/	/

V				
E	/	/	/	:‖

The suspended fourth

Here the 3rd is suspended and replaced with the 4th degree of the scale. All six primary chords in a key can be turned into suspended forms, although these are not all of the same kind if the sus4 is drawn purely from the scale. However, although IV and bVII need off-scale notes (b7 and b3 of the scale respectively) these are common notes in blues-inflected harmony, so it is acceptable to use them.

I	II	III	IV	V	VI	bVII
Gsus4	Asus4	Bsus4	Csus4	Dsus4	Esus4	Fsus4 (with a Bb)

The 'sus4' is dramatic, focused, assertive, extravert where the sus2 is introvert, and very tense. It tolerates distortion, so is an ideal chord for guitar rock. Acoustic singer-songwriters value it as a decoration of the major or minor chord with the same root. It serves effectively at transitions between song sections, especially build-ups (a Springsteen speciality). It also features in riffs, and combines with fifth chords to extend passages that need to be tonally neutral (neither major nor minor).

Springsteen songs that feature chord I as a sus4 include 'Mary's Place', 'Night', 'No

Surrender' (all Fsus4), 'Two Hearts' (where the driving riff is C-Csus4), 'The Fuse' (D-Dsus4 verse), 'Be True' (A-Asus4 after chorus), 'Born To Run' and 'She's The One' (the riffs themselves imply an Esus4). 'Wages of Sin' starts with an Esus4. 'None But The Brave' in E uses an Asus2 (chord IV) several times in its verse and chorus. 'Dancing In The Dark' has chord V as a sus4 in its chorus for the word "fire".

The songs use sus4s in minor key contexts also. 'Roulette' starts with a strongly accented Asus4 that is chord V of the key D minor. Similarly, in 'Cover Me' the last two bars of the middle-eight are F#sus4-F# (chord V of B minor); in 'Spirit In The Night', D-Dsus4 (functioning as VII) is the approach to an E minor chorus.

The badge of honour for deploying the most sus4s goes (it's no contest) to the middle-eight of 'Born To Run' which links together Dsus4, Gsus4, Asus4, Csus4 to create a sense of movement as the music goes wandering through the keys; this is at 2:12-38 ("beyond the palace").

'Mary Queen Of Arkansas' has some sus4 chords (A7sus4 and Dsus4), which lend valuable drama in an acoustic context – take note if you play solo. In the first example, an eight-bar I-IV change is made more interesting by the sus4s. The Dsus4 note G provides a common tone as an opportunity to insert a bVII chord.

Sus4 verse in A

I				I				I				I			
A	/	/	/	Asus4	/	/	/	A	/	/	/	Asus4	/	/	/

IV				IV				bVII				IV			
D	/	/	/	Dsus4	/	/	/	G	/	/	/	Dsus4	/	/	/

Using the sus4 for an intro

Sus4 chords are great for dramatic intros and links. The tension they add to a progression is especially handy at approaches to a new section. 'For You' has a long sus4 chord V build-up to its last chorus. Simply alternating with a straight chord I can also work:

Sus4 intro in D

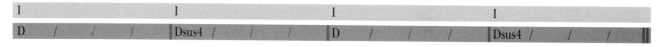

I				I				I				I			
D	/	/	/	Dsus4	/	/	/	D	/	/	/	Dsus4	/	/	/

'Mary's Place' is an example of this. In the next example the Esus4 (chord V) creates a tense expectancy of the appearance of chord I (A) which finally enters at the verse. Notice in bar 4 the suspension does not resolve on the first beat, but the third. Hanging on for another two beats is more dramatic and less predictable. In the verse a quick change to Dsus4 suggests almost a riff.

Sus4 intro / build-up in A

V	V	V	V	V
Esus4 / / /	Esus4 / / /	Esus4 / / /	Esus4	E /

[verse]

I	IV	I	I	V
A / / /	D / Dsus4 D	A / / /	A /	E :

The sus2 and sus4 together

The sus2 and sus4 chords combine naturally. This could mean either on the same chord (C-Csus2-Csus4) or on a pair of chords such as I-IV (i.e. Csus4-Fsus2). 'Brilliant Disguise' has A-Asus2 Asus4 for its intro / verse, echoing 1960s band The Searchers' 'Needles and Pins'. See also 'Rosalita', which has Fsus4 and sus2 on its intro, and 'Take 'Em As They Come' (D Dsus4 D Dsus2 riff) in this respect. Listen for sus2 and sus4 chords on A and D toward the end after 2:04 of 'Don't Look Back'.

One subtle point to observe about chord I as a sus2 and V as a sus4 is that they are the same notes in a different order. In 'Sad Eyes' chord I is Esus2 E F# B and chord V is Bsus4 B E F#. This means these chords are closely related in terms of sound and sometimes merely changing a bass note will make one sound like the other. A further handy tip is that the combination of sus2/sus4 on a single chord can be used to imply the progression I-IV-I-V as in this intro and verse idea: (where F Fsus4 F Fsus2 is a substitute for F Bbsus2 F Csus4).

Sus2/sus4 intro in F

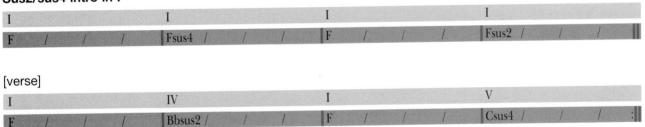

I	I	I	I
F / / /	Fsus4 / / /	F / / /	Fsus2 / /

[verse]

I	IV	I	V
F / / /	Bbsus2 / / /	F / / /	Csus4 / / :

The add 4

It is possible to create an 'add 4' chord by including both the 3rd *and* the 4th in a major chord. Cadd4 would have the notes C E F G (Csus4 is C F G). This is a major chord, not a neutral one, because it does have the 3rd. What tension it does possess is caused by the semitone proximity of the 3rd and the 4th. Without the help of an open string such a chord is difficult on the guitar, so add4 chords tend to occur on just a few pitches that have easy shapes. Springsteen included this chord in some of his folk-oriented material around the time of *The Ghost Of Tom Joad*. 'The Big Muddy' and 'Straight Time' also have Dadd4. 'Sad Eyes' has the Dadd4 shape as a guitar arpeggio riff on the intro. This chord lends powerful tension to the song 'Empty Sky', where it seems to be played with 'dropped D' tuning.

The major sixth

The major sixth chord makes one significant contribution to a Springsteen song and that's in one of his chart hits, 'Dancing In The Dark'. On the intro and the verse we hear the change B to B6. The bass note stays on B. B6 consists of the notes B D# F# G#. Chord VI in B major is G#m: G# B D# (and G#m7 would add an F#). These are closely related chords. By making the change B-B6 the song gives something of the I-VI major-minor change but stays more hopeful. The proper I-VI B-G#m change is saved until the last four bars of the verse.

This is a way of withholding chord VI but hinting at it. This is a chord relationship which, like 7ths and inversions, could be used in a three-chord trick to make the three chords go further. (For a rocked-up version of 'Dancing', which kicks the original into the long grass, check out the live cut on *Live In Barcelona*.)

The add ninth

This is the most popular of the ninth chords, partly because of its sound and as it is available in an easy fingering. It is a staple chord of breezy, radio-friendly American rock. The add ninth strengthens a simple sequence of majors. It is closely related to the sus2. Compare Csus2 (CDG) with Cadd9 (CEGD) . The latter keeps the 3rd, which makes it clear that the add9 chord is a *major* chord, not a neutral one like the sus2. This chord is called an add9 to distinguish it from the full major ninth (CEGBD).

The add9 chord is closely related to the sus2 and is a handy way to strengthen a simple sequence. Add9 chords are more popular on the guitar than full ninths because they're easier to find in a playable shape and their sound is more suited to rock music. Here's a standard I-IV change decorated with add9s, a frequent Springsteen idea:

Add9 change in C

I				I				IV				IV			
C	/	/	/	Cadd9	/	/	/	Fadd9	/	/	/	Fadd9	/	/	/ :

Add9s are often used in situations where the ninth itself is a common tone with the preceding or following chord. There is a simple explanation: it means the guitarist doesn't have to lift their finger off the note!

Add9 change in D

I				bVII				IV				II			
D	/	/	/	Cadd9	/	/	/	Gadd9	/	/	/	Em7	/	/	/ :

Cadd9 features in 'Gloria's Eyes', 'My Beautiful Reward' (where it is important to the resigned sad atmosphere), 'Wild Billy's Circus Story', 'Stolen Car'; 'My Love Will Not Let You Down' has Fadd9 in C (along with Csus4), 'My Best Was Never Good Enough' has Fadd9 and the C shape with the note G at the top, 'Factory has Fadd9' in C, '4th Of July, Asbury Park (Sandy)' has Cadd9 and Fadd9, 'Atlantic City' has a Dbadd9 (actually Cadd9 shape but with a capo at I) and 'Growin' Up' has Cadd9-Fadd9-G with the note G at the top all the time.

Another trick is to take simple I-IV-V chord changes and turn them into sequences that combine 5ths with add9s:

Fifth and add9 change in C

I				IV				V				IV			
C5	/	/	/	Fadd9	/	/	/	Gadd9	/	/	/	Fsus2	/	/	/ :||

Inversions

Inversions are another method for getting more 'mileage' out of the chords in your song. All an inversion means is a change of bass note under the chords.

In any simple major (or minor) chord there are three notes. G major consists of the notes G B D. The note after which the chord is named is called the 'root' note. The middle note is called the 'third' (because it is the 3rd of the scale of G major) and the last note is known as the 'fifth' (because it is the 5th of the scale of G major). The same is true of C major (C E G) and D major (D F# A) and their respective scales. Most of the time the lowest note in the chord (and the one that is sounded by a bass instrument in the arrangement) will be the root note. Root chords are stable and confident.

However, it is possible to put either of the other notes – the 'third' or the 'fifth' – as the bass. If the third is the lowest note the chord is a 'first inversion'. If the fifth is lowest the chord is a 'second inversion'. Here are chords I, IV and V in G major, written out in their root and inverted forms, with the names underneath:

D	G	B	G	C	E	A	D	F#
B	D	G	E	G	C	F#	A	D
<u>G</u>	<u>B</u>	<u>D</u>	<u>C</u>	<u>E</u>	<u>G</u>	<u>D</u>	<u>F#</u>	<u>A</u>
Root	**1st**	**2nd**	**Root**	**1st**	**2nd**	**Root**	**1st**	**2nd**
G	**G/B**	**G/D**	**C**	**C/E**	**C/G**	**D**	**D/F#**	**D/A**
I....................			**IV**........................			**V**...........................		

Traditionally, inverted chords for the guitar are written with a slash followed by either the third or the fifth. In addition, in this book a lower case i or ii in front of the Roman numeral indicates first or second inversion.

Although G, G/B and G/D are all G chords, the two inversions have a subtle character of their own in contrast to the root chord. This means that an extra two shades of that chord 'colour' can be had from each of the three chords I, IV, and V. If chords I, IV and V are the primary colours their inversions offer slightly different shades.

The first inversion

This chord has a feeling of movement in contrast to the 'standing still' posture of a root chord. The lowest note in a first inversion chord wants to rise or fall, or walk, to the next bass note. This makes it excellent for progressions with a descending or ascending bass.

In slow ballad-type songs a carefully-placed first inversion can convey more emotion than a root chord, and function almost as a substitute for a minor chord.

Chorus in G major with first inversion

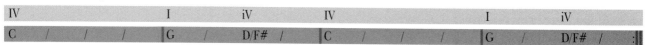

IV	I	iV	IV	I	iV
C / / /	G /	D/F# /	C / / /	G /	D/F# / :||

Inversions are crucial to the descending (and unusual) bass line of 'Walk Like A Man'. You can hear the first inversion on the second chord of the song's intro. In this song and 'Back In Your Arms' (in C: C G/B F/A Fmaj7) the descending pattern is repeated to become a turnaround with inversions. Here the F/A makes a less predictable harmonizing of the bass note A than Am would have been.

Inversions are easier to play on a keyboard, where they require only a small adjustment of the left hand position. There is a sequence of accented inversions at the end of 'Something In The Night', led by the piano. On guitar the most popular first inversion shapes are G/B and D/F#, followed by C/E and F/A. These are all in guitar-friendly keys. There are noticeably more inversions in the *Tom Joad* songs because they are naturally part of the solo folk/country style, where a singer/guitarist has to be his own bass player.

Allowing for the capo, 'Sinaloa Cowboys' has the D/F# shape, 'Balboa Park' has D/F# and C/G (a second inversion), 'The Line' has G/B. G/B is the second chord of 'All That Heaven Will Allow'. It is common to find G/B going to or from Cadd9 because they share a top note, D; as in 'Code Of Silence'. 'Cautious Man' in G uses D/F# at the end of the verse and G/B in the bridge.

'The River' has D/F# in Em. 'Brilliant Disguise' has a first inversion chord I (A/C#) in the chorus on the word "disguise".

'My City Of Ruins' (Eb F/A Bb on the "rise up" section), 'Into The Fire', 'Lonesome Day' (in the "it's all right" section joining Gm to Bb), and 'The Promise' (in its chorus of Gm F/A Bb) all have F/A. 'One Step Up' has many inversions in the bridge which help the bass-line to move down and then back up again, and a Bb-F/A-Gm change on the verse.

'Leap Of Faith' has two inversions in the chorus, on the bass line dropping going from E to B.

The second inversion

Not as assertive as the root chord, nor as mobile as the first inversion, second inversions have a dreamy quality that lends itself to impressionistic effects that work well in intros and bridges. In certain musical contexts, they serve as a point of stability more flexible than a root chord. Play this eight-bar verse and notice how bars 5-8 sound less focused than 1-4, even though the chords are in the same order:

Verse with second inversion

I				V				IV				IV			
G	/	/	/	D	/	/	/	C	/	/	/	C	/	/	/

I				iiV				iiIV				iiIV			
G	/	/	/	D/A	/	/	/	C/G	/	/	/	C/G	/	/	/

In Springsteen's music there is one specific second inversion chord which makes a vital contribution to his songs and that's the change from chord I to the second inversion of chord IV:

Verse with second inversion

I		iiIV		I		iiIV		I		iiIV		I		iiIV	
G	/	C/G	/	G	/	C/G	/	A	/	D/A	/	A	/	D/A	/

(This change can also be thought of as chord I going to a Isus4/6; the notes are the same). You can make this change gentle for quieter material or you can turn it into a grinding Stones-like riff. The chord change of A to D/A can be heard in 'Don't Look Back' (verse 2), 'Give The Girl A Kiss', 'Trouble In Paradise', 'Local Hero', 'Book Of Dreams', 'My Hometown', 'Glory Days', 'I'm A Rocker' and 'It's Hard To Be A Saint'. In other keys the change appears in G major at the start of 'Darkness On The Edge Of Town', and as B to E/B in 'Real Man', 'Leap Of Faith', and on the bridge of 'I'm A Rocker'.

Some of the common chord shapes found in Springsteen's music are illustrated in the following 30 chord boxes. The four-string shapes like F and Bsus4 are there because playing bass notes on the guitar in such a big band is less significant; the 'cut' of the guitar chords is more important, so you go for higher notes. The E5 has a droning sound that would fit a song like 'Born In The USA'. The sus2s and sus4s speak for themselves. The D/A shape creates a rhythm riff if you lift fingers 2 and 3 off and on. The D/F#, G/B, G5/D, D5, A5 and D add4 are the sort of shapes he uses when in folk singer mode. Try them when you have a capo up the neck. The F#m6 chord captures the harmony of part of 'American Skin (41 Shots)'.

CHORD SHAPES FOR SPRINGSTEEN'S SONGS

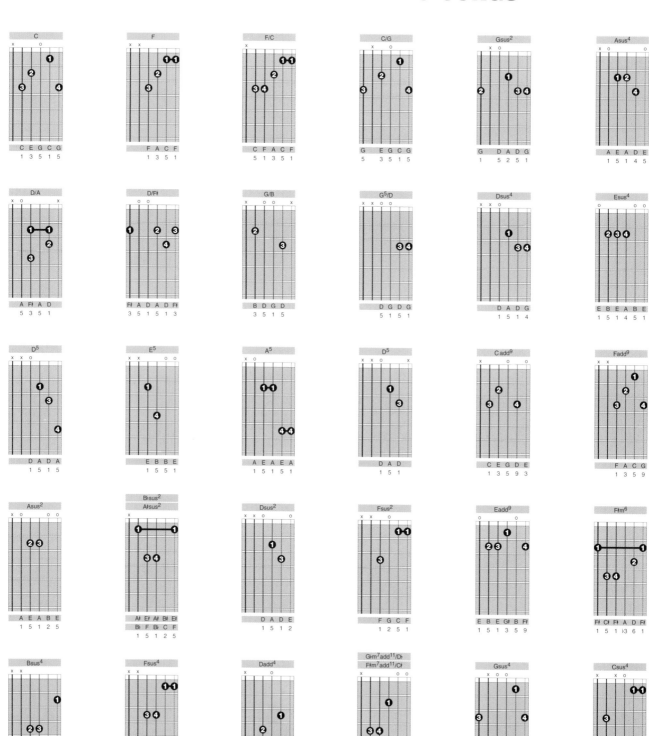

CAPO SONGS

To write songs in awkward keys on the guitar, Springsteen uses a capo (including on some of the electric songs like 'Land Of Hope And Freedom', which is less usual). The eight master chord shapes on guitar are A, C, D, E, G, Am, Dm and Em. These are the most comfortable keys in which to play. If you want to play in any other key the trick is to use a capo to find a place on the neck where the desired key becomes one of these chord shapes. So, with a capo on the first fret the 8 master-shapes are pitched at Bb, Db, Eb, F, Ab, Bbm, Ebm and Fm.

Live footage of Springsteen shows him sometimes with a capo on the guitar even where the key is not a difficult one. This is to differentiate the pitch of his guitar from that of the other guitars in the band. 'Into The Fire' would be a good example. The key is G and Van Zandt plays open chord shapes down in first position, while Bruce has a capo at the fifth fret and plays as if in D. By doing this the band get a fuller guitar sound. There would be no point in having four guitars playing the same chord in the same place.

Sometimes it is not always clear-cut which fret the capo is at because the guitar may not be at concert pitch. A number of *Nebraska* songs are roughly pitched in Db, but since they sound like a D shape it would seem Bruce had his guitar slightly below standard tuning. These songs could be played in normal tuning with a capo at the first fret and using the C shape for Db.

Here is a list of some of Springsteen's songs that use a capo, with the actual pitch followed by the shape used to give that pitch at that capo position:

Capo fret I
Lift Me Up Db = C; Further On (Up The Road) Fm = Em.

Capo fret II
The Wish A = G; Trouble River E = F#.

Capo fret III
Independence Day C = A; 'Nothing Man' Eb = C; 'When You Need Me' F = D; 'Rockaway The Days' F = D; 'Across The Border' Bb = G; 'Sinaloa Cowboys' Bb = G 'Balboa Park' Bb = G; 'One Step Up' Bb = G; 'Land of Hope and Dreams' Bb = G; 'Part Man, Part Monkey' Cm = Am; 'Paradise' Cm = Am 'Youngstown' Dm = Bm; 'Downbound Train' Gm = Em; 'Lucky Town' Gm = Em; Empty Sky Gm = Em

Capo fret IV
'Dancing In The Dark' B = G

Capo fret V
'Into The Fire' G = D, 'Pony Boy' F = C; 'The Honeymooners' C = G.

continued on next page

The Rising (live) C = G

Capo fret VII

Man At The Top G = C.

Alternate tunings

Springsteen's songs seem to make little use of alternate tunings. This is a pity because it would have enhanced the music of his most musically bare records, *Nebraska* and *The Ghost Of Tom Joad*. Alternate tunings bring out chord voicings that are not possible in standard tuning and in an acoustic context these chords can really be heard. One tuning that does crop up is 'dropped D', where the guitar's bottom E string is tuned down a tone to D. This gives anything in the key of D major a much deeper sound. Springsteen deploys this tuning for folk material and anything that requires a sludgy blues (possibly with bottleneck).

It can be heard (to my ears at least) on songs like 'Spare Parts', 'Code Of Silence', 'Souls Of The Departed', 'The Big Muddy', 'Living Proof', 'Galveston Bay', 'The New Timer', 'Straight Time', 'Blood Brothers', and 'Dead Man Walkin''. Of the last, Bruce wrote in the *Tracks* sleeve-notes, "I tuned the E string of my guitar down to a D and cut it in as low a key as possible to get as much deepness and darkness I could out of the music."

If you haven't tried alternate tunings, dropped D is a good place to start.

Technique summary for guitar

This fourth section has dealt with a variety of guitar techniques and ideas, introducing you to:

- the idea of putting the song first, the guitar second;
- playing guitar alongside keyboards;
- lead guitar techniques for your solos;
- minor 7 chords;
- sus2 and sus4 chords;
- major 6 chords;
- add9 chords;
- inversions;
- using a capo;
- using dropped D tuning.

Having looked at songwriting, guitar-playing, arrangements, and chords, there's one final important area still to discuss: lyrics.

lyrics
SECTION 5

"Most of my writing is emotionally autobiographical. You've got to pull up the things that mean something to you in order for them to mean anything to your audience. That's how they know you're not kidding." – BRUCE SPRINGSTEEN, *SONGS*

A singer needs words to sing, yet lyric-writing is something many songwriters find more difficult than composing music. So there's much to learn from an artist like Springsteen for whom the words are of vital importance, whose lyric style has changed over the years, and who is acknowledged as writing lyrics which deal with important issues.

With Springsteen it has always appeared that words are never an afterthought, secondary to the music, scribbled on the back of an envelope at the last minute just before recording, as happens in some bands. In 1974 he confessed, "A lot of the songs were written without any music at all – it's just that I do like to sing the words!" He came to prominence, in the early 1970s, dogged by a 'new Dylan' tag – a comparison he drew partly because of his vocal style at that time but more because of the lyrics. There's no doubt that, like many other rockers, Springsteen was inspired by what Dylan had done with the popular song lyric. Dylan had expanded its imagery, its rhythms and rhymes, its complexity, and its reach. In 1980 Springsteen enthused, "Bob Dylan's music is the greatest ever written, to me. The man says it all, exactly the right way. Incredibly powerful. You don't get no more intense."

On an advert for *Greetings From Asbury Park, N.J.* Springsteen's record company proudly proclaimed, "This man puts more thoughts, more ideas and images into one song than most people put into an album", before quoting lines from 'Blinded By The Light'. In his book, *Songs*, Springsteen reveals that for his debut he wrote the lyrics first and then set them to music. On the first and second albums Springsteen's lyric writing is at its most exuberant. These lyrics are characterised by a wealth of imagery and metaphor, long lines, internal rhyme (rhymes within a line instead of at the end), and rhyme schemes that use the same rhyme sound three or four times. A good example of internal rhyme is, "Everything *stops*, you hear five quick *shots*, / The *cops* come up for air" (from 'Lost In The Flood') and "I was open to *pain* and crossed by the *rain* and I walked on a crooked crutch" ('Growin' Up'). Springsteen used polysyllabic rhyme, like "urgency / emergency" ('For You'), and unusual words (like "calliope" in 'Blinded By The Light').

The lines are so long and full that at times Springsteen can only just fit them into the musical space, as with the gabbled line, "We were both hitch-hikers but you had your ear tuned to the roar / Of some metal-tempered engine on an alien, distant shore" ('For You'). But this comes over as a touching exuberance rather than a technical fault. The wordiness of the lyrics becomes part of the moving complexity of feeling with which the singer addresses the women in songs like 'For You' and 'Mary Queen Of Arkansas'. He seems inspired by them and exasperated with them simultaneously. It's a rare quality among singer-songwriters: the ability to arraign the subject of their romantic disappointment, sounding affectionate and hacked-off at the same time. He's arguing with them, yet still affectionate. It makes them, and him, seem more real.

Springsteen showed a talent for the simple but evocative phrase that describes the physical reality of a person or event. So there's the reference to "your *soft hulk* is reviving" in 'Mary Queen Of Arkansas', or the girls in '4th Of July, Asbury Park (Sandy)' who "all promise to *unsnap* their jeans", or the comment in 'For You', "that medal you wore on your chest always got in the way" where "got in the way" prompts us to think "got in the way of what?" And presumably the answer is: their love-making. Here intimacy is revealed by indirection.

There are flashes of wit, too. In 'Lost In The Flood' a biker dies in a motorcycle accident: "And there's nothin' left but some blood where the body fell / That is, nothin' that you could sell" – where the qualifying "that is" gives an abrupt, unsentimental slant on the tragedy. Likewise, in '4th Of July, Asbury Park (Sandy)', we find the witty "the cops finally busted Madame Marie / For telling fortunes better than they do", and in 'For You' the protagonist says of the subject "your life was one long emergency".

Rolling out the words

So from Bruce's early lyrics you can take the following suggestions for an approach:

- Write about the place you know but transform it in your imagination;
- Give place-names a twist so they seem more interesting;
- Write about people you know but disguise them with new names;
- Write about yourself but merely as one of a group of people whose lives are intertwined;
- Use rhyme within a line as well as at the end;
- Use a rhyming dictionary to give you multiple rhymes for a word;
- Write longer lines than you normally do;
- Use metaphors and similes to describe by comparison;
- Listen to the sound of words as well as their meaning;
- Don't be afraid to combine poetic images with colloquial phrases.

Cutting back the words

Shifting musical ambition and the Dylan comparisons eventually impelled Springsteen to make his lyrics more direct. This cutting back is first felt on *Born To Run*. The lyrics are edited to match the streamlining of his music as it shed the jazz/funk tinges and became more rock. The lines shorten, the rhymes are cut back, the imagery is more direct, almost at times filmic, as in the famous opening of 'Thunder Road': "the screen door slams / Mary's dress waves". But there are still genuinely poetic phrases like "the lonely cool before dawn", and in 'Backstreets' "one soft infested summer".

Thereafter, Springsteen's songs are less concerned with evoking moods and visual images, more concerned with telling stories and sketching characters' predicaments. This is still skilful but in a different way. A line like "And for my 19th birthday I got a union card and a wedding coat" (from 'The River') is full of compressed experience. He is able to write lines that have a plain-speaking aphoristic power, such as 'I can't tell my courage from my desperation' in 'Local

Hero', which show discrimination, or that describe human evasions, as in 'Born In The USA', where the refinery turns down the veteran's request for a job with "son if it was up to me". Imagery takes on a deeper symbolic force – like the footsteps in the sand and the shadowy elm, "the long black limousine and the mystery ride" in 'Walk Like A Man'. By the late 1980s Springsteen was extending his range to write songs about love in its later, domestic stages, as opposed to the romantic pursuit of the early songs, and then in *The Ghost Of Tom Joad* to tell the story of social outcasts and the dispossessed in the southwest states.

His lyric-writing has many virtues but it has patches blighted by one particular cliché, which can be summed up in three dangerous words: "pretty", "little" and "girl". So we find "All the little pretties" ('Tenth Avenue Freeze-Out'), "I met a little girl" ('Stolen Car'), "Hey, little girl, is your Daddy home?" ('I'm On Fire'), "And drove that little girl away" ('Racing In The Streets'), "little girl" ('Promised Land'), "Hey, little girl" ('Darlington County'), "pretty little miss" ('Working On The Highway'), "Little girl, I wanna marry you" ('I Wanna Marry You'), "Little girl with the long blond hair" ('County Fair'). The problem is that both "little" and "girl" tend to diminish. Putting them together doubles the effect, one that is hardly suitable to apply to a grown woman. The effect is to suggest a certain dumb machismo on the part of the speaker. This is unfortunate, because it confirms the suspicions of people who are prejudiced against Springsteen's work.

Furthermore, such demeaning references sometimes introduce a note (probably unintended) of condescension.

So in 'Dancing In The Dark' the unnecessary "little" in "Worrying 'bout your little world falling apart" makes it sound as though the speaker thinks his woman's world is of no matter (she might see it differently!). Similarly, in 'Racing In The Streets' the word "pretty" in the line "And all her pretty dreams are torn" implies her dreams are not worth much and she wasn't mature enough to see through them. But again, maybe now she would rather have stayed with the dude from LA in his Camaro than with the guy who spends his evenings racing in the streets.

Checklist for improving lyrics

When you've finished a lyric put it aside for a short while and then come back to it and have another look. Ask yourself:

- Are there lines that could be improved?
- Have some of the rhymes cause the lines to seem awkwardly phrased?
- Are there any obvious clichés, like hearts that beat like drums or an emotion which cuts like a knife, or a promise to be "set free"?
- Are there any filler words like "really", "just", or "well", that can be dropped?
- Are you repeating yourself with certain images or phrases?
- Have you put in words (like "pretty" or "little") that suggest a sarcasm you don't mean toward your subject?

Influences, sources and getting ideas

I often hear songwriters say, "I can't think what to write about." There are many ways to avoid writer's block:

- You can draw ideas from singers and musicians of earlier periods;
- You can get ideas from literature, paintings and films.

Sometimes this can be just a title that you find inspiring, as Springsteen took the title of 'Thunder Road' from a Robert Mitchum film.

In 1987, in connection with *Nebraska*, Springsteen revealed, "I got into this writer, William Price Fox, who wrote *Dixiana Moon* and a lot of short stories. He's just great with detail. In 'Open All Night' I remember he had some story that inspired me." In a BBC Radio 1 interview with Trevor Dann in 1996, Bruce explained how he got into Woody Guthrie in his late twenties and early thirties when he "went back to a lot of the great country music and folk music: Hank Williams stuff, gospel music … just all kinds of American roots music that was real sustaining for me and spoke to me for one reason or another. And then just short story writers, James M. Cain, Jim Thompson, Flannery O'Connor … and films too. American film noir and stuff from out of the past … and John Ford pictures." *The Ghost Of Tom Joad* draws of course on John Steinbeck's classic novel, *The Grapes Of Wrath* (1939).

- You can take images and themes from mythology or works like the Bible. You don't necessarily have to be writing a mythological or religious song.

Western culture was once steeped in Greek and Roman myth, in classical epics like Homer's *Iliad* and *Odyssey*, or Virgil's *Aeneid* (the background to the recent film *Troy*), in the stories of Ovid's *Metamorphoses*. If the notion of getting inspiration from such sources sounds far-fetched, think of Cream's famous song 'Tales Of Brave Ulysses'. These works of literature and scripture address human emotions and conflicts which play themselves out even now in ordinary lives in ordinary places.

In this instance, it should be recalled that Springsteen, who came from a Catholic household, uses Biblical imagery and allusions in songs like 'Adam Raised A Cain', 'Gave It A Name', 'Pink Cadillac' (Adam and Eve), 'Lion's Den' (Daniel), 'The Promised Land', 'Part Man Part Monkey', 'The Price You Pay' (Moses and the chosen land), and 'Ice Man' (the flaming sword that guards the garden of Eden mentioned in *Genesis*).

For Springsteen the touchstone has long been whether a lyric illuminates a corner of human reality. In 1985 he told *Rolling Stone*, "When I sit down to write, I try to write something that feels real to me. Like, what does it feel like to be 35 or something right now, at this point in time, living in America? It's not much more conscious than that. I generally try to write songs that are about real life, not fantasy material. I try to reflect people's lives back to them in some fashion."

FIND YOUR THEMES AND IMAGES
'BORN TO RUN', 'WALK LIKE A MAN'

A songwriter/performer needs to forge an identity. This identity is comprised of many things, from a haircut and clothes to the size of your band (or whether you have one), the guitar you play, the way you sing, the style of your music. The themes of your lyrics provide one of the more significant strands of this identity. The things you want to write about need to find a resonance in other people's lives in some way for them to find a way into your music. You try to write as much as you can, and then develop an awareness of what might be specific images that you can make your own.

The often dismissive view about Springsteen is that he only writes songs about cars and girls. Rock'n'roll and cars have always been linked, going back to the 1950s and Chuck Berry tunes like 'No Particular Place To Go' and 'Maybelline'. The Beatles wrote 'Drive My Car' and John Lennon famously borrowed the phrase "here come ol' flat-top" from Berry in 'Come Together' – and had to pay for it. Cars also feature in early Beach Boys' tunes like 'Little Deuce Coupe', 'Don't Worry Baby' (a Bruce favourite), and 'I Get Around'. Historically, the birth of rock'n'roll coincided with a classic period of American car manufacture, when cars got bigger and more elaborately contoured with chrome and extravagant tail-lights. The pink Cadillac is as much a rock icon as blue-suede shoes or a guitar-shaped swimming pool. Out of that same 1950s milieu came the Fender Stratocaster, which looked like a space-age gizmo. They even painted Strats in car colours.

So, in Springsteen's work we find songs like 'Cadillac Ranch', 'Pink Cadillac', and 'Racing In The Streets', which starts like a car sales catalogue: "I got a '69 Chevy with a 396 / Fuelie heads and a Hurst on the floor." But as Springsteen countered, "I don't write songs about cars. My songs are about people *in* those cars." The car in his songs is usually on a journey, and it's the journey that is significant.

In 'Born To Run' everyone seems to be out in their cars – the "hemi-powered drones / scream down the boulevard". It's a more glitzy, neon-lit version of the vision that closes another of the greatest songs about America and journeys: Simon and Garfunkel's 'America', where, even on a night when Springsteen might have been spraying blues licks round a sweaty club in Asbury Park, a few miles up the road the protagonist is "counting the cars on the New Jersey turnpike". In both 'Born To Run' and 'Thunder Road' ("my car's out back") the young hero (or anti-hero) offers a ride out of a gloomy dead-end present to a better life some place else. Like the occupants of the cars in Simon and Garfunkel's song, they're all looking for America in its best sense. If it isn't that, the hero is out in the street trying to find his feminine ideal (as in 'Night') or prepared to 'Drive All Night' to see her. The cars, the journey and the road are metaphors for life's quest.

In 'The Promise' someone else is listening to "the tyres swish past in the rain". This song alludes back to 'Thunder Road' as 'The Ghost Of Tom Joad' alludes back to 'Born To Run': "the highway is alive tonight / But ain't nobody kidding no one about where it goes." If you have written enough songs you can eventually allude to some of your older tunes and re-comment on their lyric themes. Until you get an audience that knows them this won't be obvious to anyone but yourself – but it's another way of getting fresh inspiration.

Eventually Springsteen realised he had to deal with what happens when you can't travel anymore and you have to find a place to stop. Thus, in 'Racing In The Streets' the speaker "blew that Camaro off my back / And drove that little girl away" but now they're older and sadder "she cries herself to sleep at night". And most profound of all, in 'Walk Like A Man' the car becomes a metaphor for commitment and the uncertainties of the future, as Springsteen describes "The handsome groom and his bride / As they stepped into that long black limousine / For their mystery ride."

So, as you write lyrics, watch out for unwanted repetition of images, but see if there are distinctive images and themes to which you unconsciously return which can be made yours.

REDRAFTING A LYRIC
'STOLEN CAR'

Sometimes a lyric needs cutting back and re-focusing. It may be that you have said too much about the story, the emotion, or the characters. It can be more effective to have some things unsaid, or to leave things open to the listener's imagination. If you have already set the words to music, that may also need to be cut. Don't be afraid to be ruthless.

Nothing in Springsteen's catalogue illustrates this better than the two versions of 'Stolen Car'. This haunting song was originally released on *The River*, where it closed side three of the vinyl double. However, the 4-CD box set *Tracks* has another, earlier version with a lyric twice as long and different music. It is fascinating to compare the two.

The final 'Stolen Car' is a brooding nocturne that smells of gasoline and a cold night wind. The instrumentation is mainly rhythm guitar and piano, with a low rumble of drums (probably timpani) every now and then. Sustained notes sung as backing vocals feature on the second chorus, and a brighter synth comes in for the coda once the vocal is complete. This version has two verses and two choruses only. Until the coda there are only three chords – G (chord I), C (chord IV) and C/G (a second inversion IV). Almost at the fade the music suddenly plunges onto a poignant Em (chord VI) followed by a passing D (chord V) in the keyboard. Musically, this 'Stolen Car' is minimal and restrained.

Lyrically, this is a confessional piece in which a man describes the failure of his marriage. The majority of songs in popular music are about wanting love and/or chasing it. Few deal with what happens once you get it. Springsteen compresses the whole romantic pursuit into the first two lines: "I met a little girl and I settled down / In a pretty little house on the edge of town." You can turn this into a technique for taking a lyric into uncharted territory:

• Imagine a situation that would have taken up a whole lyric, condense it into a few lines and then carry the story on from there.

By the end of the first verse, a mere two lines later, the characters in 'Stolen Car' find their promises failing: "And little by little we drifted from each other's heart." Verse two tries to find a reason for it. Then comes the chorus, in which the protagonist declares "I'm driving a stolen car." It's a cry for help. He waits to get caught but ironically never does. Recall the colloquial expression that sums up uselessness: he couldn't get himself arrested. Verse three voices his wife's sorrow, as she asks him if he could remember the love-letters he wrote to her, the legacy of an emotion now gone. Then we're into the last chorus where he tries to reassure himself but laments that "I travel in fear / That in this darkness I will disappear." The protagonist comes face to face with what is his underlying existential fear, one made worse by the failure of his marriage. His own nihilism is whispering in his ear; he is terrified of losing himself.

The lyric leaves the story there. We don't know whether he did eventually get arrested, or whether he patched up his marriage, or left his wife. By comparison, the earlier, longer draft of 'Stolen Car' doesn't have the same power, either musically or lyrically. Musically, it's a band song for a subject where a band wasn't necessary. It uses more chords in a longer structure that includes a bridge. Lyrically, it has a long sequence in which the protagonist, who has actually left his wife, is looking at the lights of a distant party across a river and wondering whether she is looking for him. He describes having a dream in which he re-lives his marriage ceremony. The final chorus describes his feeling of invisibility: "nobody ever sees me as I ride by".

To get the final 'Stolen Car', Springsteen had to do a lot of work, cutting and re-setting and re-imagining this situation. It's an important lesson in realising that sometimes a songwriter has to be ready to look again at a song to find its very best form. And if in doubt, cut.

WRITING A 'MESSAGE' LYRIC
THE RISING

It may be that you see so many things wrong with the world that you are never short of things to write about. Perhaps you want to write songs which have an element of protest about them. Perhaps you want to write songs with a message.

Beware, this is harder than it seems. Few traps are so powerfully sprung on the unwary songwriter as when he or she tries to write a 'protest' song or a song that has a 'message'. And having strong opinions about life, love, the government, TV or the ecology is no guarantee that you will be able to write a good lyric about these things.

'Message' songs are bywords for trite collections of slogans, platitudes and generalised sentiment with neither artistic validity nor imaginative power. The very idea of writing a song with a 'message' is itself flawed. It implies once you get the message you can throw away the song as if it were no more than a sweet wrapper. But any art that has value will keep you coming back to it, again and again. If it's art of any value you can never throw it aside even when you get the message.

Springsteen faced this specific lyric problem many times. His writing gives important hints about how to overcome it. The controversy over 'Born In The USA' is a salutary warning about how a lyric can be misinterpreted. As he said in 1987, "It's not that people aren't taught to think, but that they're not taught to think hard enough. 'Born In The USA' is not ambiguous. All you got to do is listen to the verses. If you don't listen to the verses, you're not gonna get the whole song, you're just gonna get the chorus."

Particularise, specify, humanise

Many Springsteen songs have spot-lit social injustice, unemployment, poverty, crime, and how these blight peoples' lives. He has also taken on the creationists in 'Part Man, Part Monkey' and the state of US television in '57 Channels (And Nothing On)'.

In his early songs he was an observer, watching the police have shoot-outs in the street. In recent years he has sympathetically tried to enter the wasted lives of those who live in dereliction, and sing about them from the individual's perspective looking outward. The young man who observed the guy who gets "blown right off his feet" in 'Lost In The Flood' becomes the mature songwriter who humanises the protest of 'American Skin (41 Shots)' by the touching device of having the mother ask her son to promise to behave correctly if he is approached by a policeman.

So here's the first tip: if you want to write about an issue, you have to find a way to embody it in a particular situation with specific details. It's the specific detail and point-of-view which humanises the general issue. You have to show how a single person could be affected in order to make the listener relate it to themselves. This may involve writing the song from the angle of someone else, not yourself.

In an interview with *Uncut* in 2002, Springsteen explained that when dealing with these bigger topics, "The secret of the songwriting was to get personal first, then you sort of shade in universal feelings. That's what balances the songs. All experience is personal so you have to start there, and then if you can connect in what's happening with everyone, the universality of an experience, then you're creating that alchemy where your audience is listening to it, they're hearing what they're feeling inside and they're also feeling 'I'm not alone.'"

Oblique meanings

Sometimes a song can deal with a serious topic through its imagery and by indirection, rather than by confronting the topic directly. This can be more powerful for the listener because it leaves them room to find their way to the topic, instead of being hit over the head with it. The more highly-charged and emotive the topic, the more this approach is valuable, and may become the only way of responding to avoid traps like insensitivity or sentimentality.

Topics don't come more highly-charged than terrorist attacks. The events of 9/11 presented any songwriter with as big a challenge as you could imagine. Springsteen's response was *The Rising*, a bold and adventurous record which avoided pitfalls that would have claimed many a lesser talent.

Some of the songs that most seemed to be about 9/11 had in fact been written before, such as 'My City Of Ruins'. But they fitted in an oblique way. In the light of that event they took on new meanings. Change the context and sometimes you change the song. This seemed to give Springsteen the clue to how a group of songs could be about something general without being slogans and without losing touch with the individual.

About the album he said, "It's not necessarily linear and it's not necessarily directly literal … That was something I was trying not to do. I wanted to feel emotionally in that context but not directly literal, though on some songs I was gonna be more literal than others … This album is the opposite end of the lyrical spectrum [to *Joad*]. There's detail, but it was a different type of writing than I've done in a while. It was just sort of pop song writing or rock song writing, y'know? I was trying to find a way to tell that context.

"One of the things I learnt on some of my earlier records where I tried to record the band … for instance, on *Nebraska*, immediately the band played those songs they over-ruled the lyrics. It didn't work. Those two forms didn't fit. The band comes in and generally makes noise, and the lyrics wanted silence, y'know? They make arrangement, and the lyrics wanted less arrangement. The lyrics wanted to be at the centre and there was a minimal amount of music … So with *The Rising* I was trying to make an exciting record with the E Street Band which I hadn't done in a long time, so that form was kind of driving me … [The lyrics] work because they're embedded in music that is very life-affirming. That balance has been something I think I've struck in all my best songs, like my verses are always the blues and my choruses are gospel."

In other words, the meaning of a lyric is not just a matter of words. It is also affected by the music that is its context.

Words and music

This is a dimension of the relation of words to music that songwriters need to remember, especially if writing a song that addresses big issues. Simple or indirect language can be highly charged by the music. The music can add emotion to quite plain statements; then you don't have to spell out the emotion.

A good example is the little-known 'The Honeymooners', which includes some finely-observed domestic detail about a marriage and two families drawing closer, but also has a dramatic musical twist up its sleeve.

The lyric is sung over chords I, IV and V. After the vocal ends, keyboards enter, and bring with them two minor chords (II and III) that stand out like thunderhead clouds on a bright sunny day. Was this a way of saying that there is pain ahead for the newly-weds, even as they celebrate their union? Whether that was intentional or not, those minor chords change our perception of the lyric.

LEAVE THEM GUESSING: THE INCONCLUSIVE LYRIC
'CAUTIOUS MAN', 'IF I SHOULD FALL BEHIND'

Your lyrics should always make sense, but they needn't give away all the information about a story or a situation that a listener might like. Sometimes it is appropriate to tell part of a story only.

Springsteen once said, "The songs I write, they don't have particular beginnings and they don't have endings. The camera focuses in and then out." He has many later songs that embrace the inconclusiveness and uncertainties of relationships. Two such are 'Cautious Man' and 'If I Should Fall Behind'.

In the former, the central character is Bill Horton, "a cautious man of the road". Cleverly, Springsteen gives him a physical mannerism of looking over his shoulder to capture his wariness toward life itself. In verse two, Bill meets May and they fall in love. He lets go of his caution. In verse three, we are told he has love and fear tattooed on his hands. They marry, he builds a house. Verse four explains how Bill wants the marriage to succeed and works at it. He prays for help because he knows "in a restless heart the seed of betrayal lay". In verse five he awakes from a bad dream. He gets up and goes to the road and finds nothing but miles and emptiness. In the last verse he is afflicted by a sense of cold and there is a reminder of the words tattooed on his knuckles. The song ends with the gesture of him brushing "the hair from his wife's face" in the moon-light, which in a memorable image is "filling their room in the beauty of God's fallen light". The light is divine but fallen, imperfect – like people.

We know at this moment Bill Horton has a revelation of the value of what he possesses. But whether it will be enough to keep them together we do not know. 'Cautious Man' is more interesting as a lyric than as a song. The music adds little – the melody is linear, the harmony conservative, the arrangement plain. Only after verse 3 does the keyboard bring the first hint of a fourth chord (III) into a three-chord trick.

The defining image

Always be alert to an image or symbol that will somehow capture in an instant what the song is about. 'Cautious Man' does just this.

Springsteen told *Q* in 1992, "If you go back to 'Cautious Man' on *Tunnel Of Love*, about the guy who has love and fear tattooed on his hands – that's about the story for most people. There's a world of love there and there's a world of fear too and it's standing right in front and very often that fear feels a lot realer and certainly more urgent than the feeling of love. The night my son was born, I got close to a feeling of a real, pure, unconditional love with all the walls down. All of a sudden, what was happening was so immense that it just stomped all the fear away for a little while and I remember feeling overwhelmed. But I also understood why you're so frightened. When that world of love comes rushing in, a world of fear comes in with it." Few rock singers have been able to articulate this sense of competing feelings in their songs.

Musically more successful is 'If I Should Fall Behind', which also has a lyric about the uncertainties of the future. This is not written as a narrative but as a first person statement. A couple stand on the verge of marriage, facing the anxieties of commitment. Where romantic songs stress the likeness of lovers, this one embraces the fact of difference. In verse two Springsteen sings with a hard-won maturity, "But each lover's steps fall so differently". In the bridge the song addresses the fact that everyone "dreams of a love lasting and true" but that dream doesn't always survive contact with reality. Instead, they can at least "make our steps clear so the other may see". The last verse evokes pastoral Biblical imagery of a river in the valley ahead, the oak tree, the path of life and the threat of mortality, "Should we lose each other in the shadow of the evening trees". The beauty of the hook, "if I should fall behind wait for me", is the way it recognises human frailty. It portrays marriage as a journey not a destination, thus neatly avoiding a negative reaction of envy from the listener.

These two songs (and there are many others in his work) show that a successful lyric does not have to be a lyric of answers or clear-cut beginnings and endings. The incomplete lyric allows space for the imagination of the listener to come forward and fill the space left unwritten.

ANOTHER 'I': LET SOMEONE ELSE SPEAK
'MEETING ACROSS THE RIVER'

If you get bored or tired with telling your own story, why not tell someone else's? And to make it dramatic, tell it from their point of view.

Point of view is always important in a lyric. Many songs are written in first person confessional style, where the "I" of the song is you. This can put a strain on the songwriter if they feel too exposed or run out of experiences to write about. Another option is to be less direct and more fictional. You can make the "I" someone else (as Springsteen does in the 'The River' and 'Born In The USA'), or you can address a "you" which could be someone else or could be self-referential (as in 'The Price You Pay') where you have a dialogue with yourself, or you can write in third person telling a story, as Springsteen does in many of the *Tom Joad* songs.

The point of view could also come from someone a different age to yourself. In *Songs* Springsteen wrote of *Nebraska*, "I often wrote from a child's point of view. 'Mansion On The Hill', 'Used Cars', 'My Father's House' – these were all stories that came directly out of my experience with my family."

Producer Chuck Plotkin once said, "Bruce's gift is to locate the heart in some character's dilemma." Springsteen is very good at narrative songs. One of the best is 'Meeting Across The River' (from *Born To Run*) where he presents a character in a 'dramatic monologue', talking not to us but to another character who is also part of the story. What results is an overheard conversation of unintended self-revelation. The "I" is trying to put across a certain image of himself to Eddie, but we are forming a different opinion. It's a complex effect, beautifully executed.

In this scenario a small-time crook talks to his friend about a "job", for which he needs to borrow money and take a drive through the tunnel to the other side of the city. Eddie can come along but has to promise not to talk. This indicates that the speaker looks down on him, or at least doesn't trust him. The speaker says the guy they are going to meet is "the real thing" and "doesn't dance" – a euphemism for 'mess about'. The speaker has heard this is their last chance – which implies they have been unsuccessful before. We know the speaker is desperate, and doesn't have a car or money.

Verse three alludes to the "job" and how if it gets "blown" they will end up in trouble – and Eddie is warned he'll be in trouble too – perhaps unlike previous occasions. All they have to do is "hold up our end" (whatever that precisely means), and here Springsteen adds a delightful interjection by the speaker – "here stuff this in your pocket / It will look like you're carrying a friend" (ie, a gun). So they are not actually carrying firearms. The speaker tells him not to smile and to change his shirt because tonight "we got style".

There is also a troubled love relationship described between the speaker and a woman called Cherry who is angry and threatening to leave him for selling her radio to a pawn shop. He then tries to justify himself to Eddie by saying that the money for the "job" ($2000) is "practically sitting here in my pocket".

The final verse gives his sense of what will happen and how everything will go right. He imagines himself returning to their lodging, throwing the money down to show her he wasn't just talking "this time" (implying that on other occasions he has been) and then he'll go out for a walk. He has drifted off from the business in hand and has to pull himself back to reality with the last line, asking again if Eddie can give him a lift.

We never know exactly what they were going to do, whether it worked or whether they got away with it. But we feel we know these people and something of their past and present. It is a fine realisation of characters in a situation full of implied detail.

Creating a character

To write a lyric in this form, answer these questions about your character:

- Who is this person? What is their age, sex, social position, etc?
- Do they have a significant weakness or strength?
- If something is bothering them – what is it?
- What are they concerned about?
- What do they want to change?
- Where have they been and where are they going?
- How do they see the past, present and future?
- If they are talking to someone, who is it and what is the relationship?
- If they are about to do something, what is it and what will be the likely result?

Afterword

Music is a mysterious thing and not all of it can be described and schematised. It is important to understand this. Music has different dimensions. It has body and spirit, and it's often impossible to tell where one ends and the other begins. That so many contrasted songs can be composed with so few chords only goes to prove that there is a particular sense in which the formal aspects of songs – the structures, chords and rhythms – are a bit like ropes that tether a full-size balloon to the ground: they're not the balloon itself. Remember this and you will understand why the essence of Springsteen's music (or anyone else's) cannot be measured and packaged. You will also take heart and gain confidence in using for your own songs forms that have been taken by countless others. The craft is the mooring ropes – the 'balloon' (if it comes), the inspiration, will be yours and yours alone.

Think of it like this. When Bruce Springsteen sits down to write a song and fingers the chords E and A they're his E and A and they're the E and A of that particular song. If I sit down to write a song they're my E and A in that song of mine. And if *you* write a song they're the E and A of that specific song of yours.

Revising a song

Songwriting Secrets has covered most of the major areas of the songwriting craft – structures, chords, arrangements and lyrics. One of the most important techniques a songwriter can learn is the art of revision. This can apply to all aspects of a song. Here's a checklist:

- Could the song be longer, or shorter? Or is it the right length?
- Could you make the intro more interesting?
- Does the song have enough rhythm?
- Does the song have the right tempo? Should it be quicker, or slower?
- Do the various sections flow into each other smoothly?
- Could you add drama by delaying any section by a few bars?
- If your first chorus has repeats could it be improved by shortening it?
- Would the bridge be more effective if it was in a different key?
- Do you have enough choruses at the end, or too many?
- Does the song have an interesting end?
- Is the song in the right key for your voice?

I hope you have enjoyed tracing the connections between the common tradition of songwriting and the specific uses to which Bruce Springsteen put these ideas in his own songs. It was my intention that this book should take readers deeper into Springsteen's music, and deeper into their own and the music they may write in the future.

Springsteen took the rock'n'roll torch from the singers, bands, and writers he admired and added something of himself to it as he passed it on in his recordings and concerts. There is much humanity in his work. In *Songs* there's an expressive photo of him sitting on a bed with his guitar, long before he ever made a record, fingering a chord and searching for a life in music. There are young people out there now doing the same. I hope this book helps them find their own songwriting secrets.

extras

A BRUCE SPRINGSTEEN DISCOGRAPHY

GREETINGS FROM ASBURY PARK, N.J. (1972)

Blinded By the Light / Growin' Up / Mary Queen of Arkansas / Does This Bus Stop At 82nd Street? / Lost In The Flood / The Angel / For You / Spirit In The Night / It's Hard To Be A Saint In The City

SPRINGSTEEN: *"I got a lot of things out in that first album. I let out an incredible amount at once – a million things in each song. They were written in half-hour, 15-minute blasts. I don't know where they came from. A few of them I worked on for a week or so, but most of them were just jets, a real energy situation."*

Signed as a solo singer-songwriter by John Hammond, Springsteen insisted on making a record with a band backing him. This results in a good balance of acoustic guitars with the rhythm section. A strong set of songs, stuffed full of imagery, is sung in Springsteen's young, most pliable voice. The production may not be top-notch but this is music with a generous, all-embracing spirit. It includes 'Mary Queen Of Arkansas', a dramatic acoustic ballad superior in strictly musical terms to anything on *Nebraska* or *The Ghost Of Tom Joad*, and songs like 'Blinded By The Light' and 'For You', which were hits for Mannfred Man's Earth Band and Greg Kihn.

THE WILD, THE INNOCENT AND THE E STREET SHUFFLE (1973)

The E Street Shuffle / 4th of July, Asbury Park (Sandy) / Kitty's Back / Wild Billy's Circus Story / Incident On 57th Street / Rosalita (Come Out Tonight) / New York City Serenade

SPRINGSTEEN: *'We were just sitting there, flashing on everything that was happening. I was exactly where I wanted to be. I had a band. I knew who I was. We were getting work. The album reflects that."* *(1980) "When I went on the road, I took the point of view I developed on my first record and I began to write with the band in mind, with the idea of mixing those two things." (1999) "It only lasted for a very brief period. The next record was Born To Run and it was immediately less eccentric." (1999)*

The Wild, The Innocent and the E Street Shuffle is a festival of delight. At this time Springsteen was playing a kind of funk-rock, and the soul influence adds a glow to the music. Every song teems with local colour, characters, places, almost like little novellas, and the music has the invention and colour to match. These songs are as sensual as the experience of being out on the street in early morning sunshine with the smell of coffee and the traces of last night's perfume. It is as if Springsteen had re-invented The Band's mid-1960s sound: it rocks but it's light on its feet, bursting with sheer musicality. Eccentric or not, for some this is Bruce's finest hour.

BORN TO RUN (1975)

Thunder Road / Tenth Avenue Freeze-out / Night / Backstreets / Born To Run / She's The One / Meeting Across The River / Jungleland

SPRINGSTEEN: *"When I did* Born To Run, *I thought, 'I'm going to make the greatest rock & roll*

record ever made.'" "The only concept that was around Born To Run *was that I wanted to make a big record, you know, that sounds like these words. Just like a car, zoom, straight ahead, that when the sucker comes on it's like wide open. No holds barred!" (1978)*

Born To Run is one of the definitive rock albums inspired by the city, dramatising the romantic longings of urban life. It presented snapshots of the tenements, streets and highways, where radios blare through summer windows, bikers pose with their machines, and lovers make out on the beach. At its heart was the car and the open road, the idea of driving away together and escaping. This is most clearly caught in the famous title track, but it's all over the album, right from 'Thunder Road', with its narrative of broken-hearted boys crying over graduation gowns. Piano and glockenspiel glitter on the tracks like tarmac strewn with diamonds. No matter how desperate the characters, Springsteen's mini-*West Side Story* dreamed there was a better place at the freeway's end. Much of his career since has questioned that, but *Born To Run* is a city to visit when you need the strength to dream.

DARKNESS ON THE EDGE OF TOWN (1978)

Badlands / Adam Raised A Cain / Something In The Night / Candy's Room / Racing In The Street / The Promised Land / Factory / Streets Of Fire / Prove It All Night / Darkness on the Edge of Town

SPRINGSTEEN: *"That was a record where I spent a lot of time focusing. And what I focused on was this one idea: What do you do if your dream comes true? Where does that leave you? What do you do if that happens? And I realised part of what you have to face is the problem of isolation. You can get isolated if you've got a lot of dough or if you don't have much dough, whether you're Elvis Presley or whether you're sitting in front of the TV with a six-pack of beer. It's easy to get there." "Most of the songs were written real fast. It was just figuring out what to do with them." (1978)*

Litigation caused a hiatus in Springsteen's career after the release of *Born To Run*. Unable to continue recording, the E Street Band toured to support themselves, and Springsteen brooded over the apparent wreck of his musical dreams. His fourth album exudes dark feelings of anger, disillusionment and frustration. The production is drier-sounding than the Spectoresque *Born To Run*, and Springsteen pushes the masculinity of his new vocal style to the limit, on tracks like 'Streets Of Fire' and 'Something In The Night'. 'Factory' and 'Adam Raised A Cain' addressed his relationship with his father, but 'Candy's Room' was the musical gem for its unpredictable twists and turns.

THE RIVER (1980)

The Ties That Bind / Sherry Darling / Jackson Cage / Two Hearts / Independence Day / Hungry Heart / Out On The Street / Crush On You / You Can Look (But You Better Not Touch) / I Wanna Marry You / The River / Point Blank / Cadillac Ranch / I'm A Rocker Fade Away / Stolen Car / Ramrod / The Price You Pay / Drive All Night / Wreck On The Highway

SPRINGSTEEN: *"I did the* Darkness on the Edge of Town … *and with The River thing I allowed some light to come in, part of the time. I had to – had to. In a funny way, I felt that I didn't have the centre, so what I had to do was I had to get left and right, in hope that it would create some sort of centre – or some sense of centre."*

Recorded live in the studio, *The River* took a year to put together. The band played through some 90 songs and consumed half a million dollars in recording costs. It originated from a single LP called *The Ties That Bind*, but eventually came out as a double. Springsteen reckoned it was the first time they'd really got the band's live sound down on tape. Of the songs, half were jolly uptempo rockers and party songs, the other half more sombre. The title track, 'The River', was included in the *No Nukes* concert and film, one of his first narrative songs about workers who marry early and lose their jobs. 'Hungry Heart' was his first Top 10 single. Musically there were signs of a certain conservatism creeping in.

NEBRASKA (1982)

Nebraska / Atlantic City / Mansion On The Hill / Johnny 99 / Highway Patrolman / State Trooper / Used Cars / Open All Night / My Father's House / Reason To Believe

SPRINGSTEEN: *"I got this little cassette recorder that's supposed to be really good, plugged it in, turned it on, and the first song I did was 'Nebraska'. I just kinda sat there: you can hear the chair creaking on 'Highway Patrolman' in particular. I recorded them in a couple of days … I only had four tracks, so I could play the guitar, sing, then I could do two other things. That was it. I mixed it on this little board, an old beat-up Echoplex."*

How do you follow a double album? Springsteen demoed these songs in a few days during January 1982 at home in New Jersey. The demos included an acoustic rendition of 'Born In The USA'. The intention was for The E Street Band to record electric versions, but in the end Springsteen decided that wasn't what was needed. So what originated as a self-made four-track demo was commercially released. Around the time of *The River* he had started exploring the music of Woody Guthrie. These songs were written in a folk style, with Springsteen changing his voice yet again, this time to a thinner countryish vocal, and the songs themselves rarely have more than three chords. The minimalism of *Nebraska* has attracted much critical praise, but its reality can be felt by some to be monotonous.

BORN IN THE USA (1984)

Born In The USA / Cover Me / Darlington County / Working On The Highway / Downbound Train / I'm On Fire / No Surrender / Bobby Jean / I'm Goin' Down / Glory Days / Dancing In The Dark / My Home Town

SPRINGSTEEN: *"That was a rock record. When I put it on, that's kind of how it hits me: That's a rock record. And the bookends ['Born In The USA' and 'My Hometown'] sort of covered the thing and made it feel more thematic than probably it actually was … But I never really felt like I quite got it." (1988) "I wasn't satisfied with the 'Born in the USA' record. I did not think I made all the connections I wanted to make on it." (1987)*

Returning to electric arrangements, Springsteen presented the public with a single album of songs recorded as a band in the studio. Steve Van Zandt: "That was literally live, at least the eight or nine things we did before I left. If Bruce wanted to sing it again, we'd play it again; that's how live it was." The album yielded a number of hit singles like the brooding 'I'm On Fire' and 'Glory Days', but it was the stark power and imagery of the title track that connected Springsteen to an enormous audience and made him a global superstar. This was to prove his last studio album with the E Street Band for over a decade.

LIVE 1975-85 (1985)

Thunder Road / Adam Raised A Cain / Spirit In The Night / 4th Of July, Asbury Park (Sandy) / Paradise By The 'C' / Fire / Growin' Up / It's Hard To Be A Saint In The City / Backstreets / Rosalita (Come Out Tonight) / Raise Your Hand / Hungry Heart / Two Hearts /Cadillac Ranch / You Can Look (But You Better Not Touch) / Independence Day / Badlands / Because The Night / Candy's Room / Darkness On The Edge Of Town / Racing In The Street / This Land Is Your Land / Nebraska / Johnny 99 / Reason To Believe / Born In The USA / Seeds / The River / War / Darlington County / Working On The Highway / The Promised Land / Cover Me / I'm On Fire / Bobby Jean / My Hometown / Born To Run / No Surrender / Tenth Avenue Freeze-Out / Jersey Girl

SPRINGSTEEN: *'We all kind of sat there listening to it and sensed that it was the end of something and that next time would be different." (1987)*

After the huge success of the mid-1980s it was time for Springsteen to take stock. It was only appropriate that a band that had made such a reputation for itself as an in-concert act should be represented by a live album, and since an average Bruce concert was now three hours it could only be matched by a box set.

It supplies great versions of a variety of songs from his career up to this point, including rarities and covers such as 'Paradise By The 'C', 'Fire', 'Because The Night', 'This Land Is Your Land', 'Seeds', 'War', and 'Jersey Girl'.

TUNNEL OF LOVE (1987)

Ain't Got You / Tougher Than The Rest / All That Heaven Will Allow / Spare Parts / Cautious Man / Walk Like A Man / Tunnel Of Love / Two Faces / Brilliant Disguise / One Step Up / When You're Alone / Valentine's Day

SPRINGSTEEN: "[Tunnel of Love] … *is a rock record, but most of the stuff is mid-tempo, and it's more rhythm-oriented, very different. It was more meticulously arranged than anything I've done since Born To Run. I was into just getting the grooves." "I thought I had to reintroduce myself as a songwriter, in a very non-iconic role." (1992) "I started to write about something I'd never written about in depth before: men and women." (Songs)*

Tunnel Of Love marks a new beginning in Springsteen's career. He cut back on the electric guitar of old, substituting keyboards, and played many of the overdubs himself. It was recorded in his home studio, which was lo-tech and could pick up street noises from outside. 'Ain't Got You' uses Bo Diddley rhythm for a stripped down 1950s feel and, like 'All That Heaven Will Allow', avoids a heavy drum accompaniment.

'Tougher Than The Rest' and the title track are dominated by keyboards. 'Walk Like A Man', musically inventive, restrained but taut, with a fine lyric, is the stand-out song, along with 'One Step Up', where the music enacts the restlessness of the words. Lyrically, Springsteen turned inward to explore the stresses and strains of a man and a woman trying to relate.

HUMAN TOUCH (1992)

Human Touch / Soul Driver / 57 Channels (And Nothin' On) / Cross My Heart / Gloria's Eyes / With Every Wish / Roll Of The Dice / Real World / All Or Nothin' At All / Man's Job / I Wish I Were Blind / The Long Goodbye / Real Man / Pony Boy

SPRNGSTEEN: *"Roy [Bittan] and I started working together pretty steadily. I had a little studio in my garage, and I came up with 'Real World'. What I started to do were little writing exercises. I tried to write something that was soul oriented. Or I'd play around with existing pop structures. And that's kind of how I did the* Human Touch *record. A lot of it is generic, in a certain sense."*

Human Touch continues some of the lyric themes of *Tunnel Of Love*. It was recorded with session players and planned to be a single album. Four producers including Springsteen are credited on the record. The experimentation gives it a slightly unfocused quality and there aren't any songs to stand with the best of his past. The reception of the album was complicated because it eventually came out alongside *Lucky Town*.

LUCKY TOWN (1992)

Better Days / Lucky Town / Local Hero / If I Should Fall Behind / Leap Of Faith / The Big Muddy / Living Proof / Book Of Dreams / Souls of the Departed / My Beautiful Reward

SPRINGSTEEN: *"Then I wrote the song 'Living Proof', and when I wrote that, I said: 'Yeah, that's what I'm trying to say. That's how I feel.' And that was a big moment, because I landed hard in the present, and that was where I wanted to be. I'd spent a lot of my life writing about my past, real and imagined, in some fashion. But with* Lucky Town, *I felt like that's where I am. This is who I am. This is what I have to say. These are the stories I have to tell. This is what's important in my life right now. And I wrote and recorded that whole record in three weeks in my house."*

The song 'Living Proof' was written early in 1992 after Springsteen had listened to Dylan's 'Series Of Dreams', taken from *The Bootleg Series* box set. *Lucky Town* is a stronger set than *Human Touch*. Several tracks like 'Souls of the Departed' and 'The Big Muddy' explore a grungy detuned blues sound with slide guitar. But it also has several beautiful love songs in 'If I Should Fall Behind' and 'My Beautiful Reward'. Sometimes the singing/melody doesn't shake off a feeling of quiet unease, and the music doesn't always find a new language to express this hard-won domestic joy. 'Better Days' seems too desperately sung for its sentiment.

BRUCE SPRINGSTEEN IN CONCERT MTV PLUGGED (1992)

Red Headed Woman / Better Days / Atlantic City / Darkness on the Edge of Town / Man's Job / Human Touch / Lucky Town / I Wish I Were Blind / Thunder Road / Light Of Day / If I Should Fall Behind / Living Proof / My Beautiful Reward

His stature allowed Springsteen to cut a deal with MTV to side-step the acoustic ethos of the *Unplugged* series. So this is an electric set of recent songs with a few old favourites. The stand-out tracks are probably 'If I Should Fall Behind', and the electric arrangement of 'Atlantic City'.

GREATEST HITS (1995)

Born To Run / Thunder Road / Badlands / The River / Hungry Heart / Atlantic City / Dancing In The Dark / Born In The USA / My Hometown / Glory Days / Brilliant Disguise / Human Touch / Better Days / Streets Of Philadelphia / Secret Garden / Murder Incorporated / Blood Brothers / This Hard Land

SPRINGSTEEN: *"I like the classic idea of hits – it was sort of like 50,000,000 Elvis Fans Can't Be Wrong. That was what we were thinking when we put it out. The album was supposed to be fun, something that you could vacuum the rug to if you wanted to … I wanted to introduce my music to younger fans, who for 12 bucks could get a pretty good overview of what I've done over the years."*

As a single 'Best Of' album, the slightly mis-named *Greatest Hits* skips across Springsteen's career, taking no songs from the first two albums and only six from before *Born In The USA*.

The main point of interest was the inclusion of the award-winning 'Streets Of Philadelphia' along with four new songs recorded with the E Street Band, the first recording Springsteen had done with the guys for a decade. Intriguingly, Springsteen said that 'Secret Garden' belonged to an unreleased album he made in 1994.

THE GHOST OF TOM JOAD (1995)

The Ghost of Tom Joad / Straight Time / Highway 25 / Youngstown / Sinaloa Cowboys / The Line / Balboa Park / Dry Lightning / The New Timer / Across The Border / Galveston Bay / My Best Was Never Good Enough

SPRINGSTEEN: *"It was an acoustic album where I picked up elements of the themes I had worked on in the past and set the stories in the mid-1990s … the music was minimal; the melodies were uncomplicated, yet played an important part in the story-telling process. The simplicity and plainness, the austere rhythms defined who these characters were and how they expressed themselves."* (Songs)

Tom Joad is a character in John Steinbeck's novel *The Grapes Of Wrath*. This was Springsteen's second venture into a stripped-down acoustic sound, with minimal accompaniment and the guitar mixed low, though better-recorded than *Nebraska*. I suspect this is a record more praised than listened to. Musically these songs are not very interesting. The emphasis is on the lyrics, the characters, the story-telling. Are these themes incompatible with a more adventurous presentation? Think of the guitar-playing and/or melody that writers like Joni Mitchell, Roy Harper, John Renbourn or Nick Drake could have brought to this and you get an idea of what's missing. If Springsteen ever makes a third acoustic album it would be good to see him pick up where 'Mary Queen Of Arkansas' left off.

TRACKS (1999)

Mary Queen of Arkansas / It's Hard To Be A Saint In The City / Growin' Up / Does This Bus Stop at 82nd Street? / Bishop Danced / Santa Ana / Seaside Bar Song / Zero and Blind Terry / Linda Let Me Be The One / Thundercrack / Rendezvous / Give The Girl A Kiss / Iceman / Bring On The Night / So Young And In Love / Hearts Of Stone / Don't Look Back / Restless Nights / A Good Man Is Hard To Find (Pittsburgh) / Roulette / Dollhouse / Where The Bands Are / Loose Ends / Living On The Edge Of The World / Wages Of Sin / Take 'Em

As They Come / Be True / Ricky Wants A Man Of Her Own / I Wanna Be With You / Mary Lou / Stolen Car / Born In The USA / Johnny Bye-Bye / Shut Out The Light / Cynthia / My Love Will Not Let You Down / This Hard Land / Frankie / TV Movie / Stand On It / Lion's Den / Car Wash / Rockaway The Days / Brothers Under The Bridge ('83) / Man At The Top / Pink Cadillac / Two For The Road / Janey Don't You Lose Heart / When You Need Me / The Wish / The Honeymooners / Lucky Man / Leavin' Train / Seven / Angels / Gave It A Name / Sad Eyes / My Lover Man / Over The Rise / When The Lights Go Out / Loose Change / Trouble In Paradise / Happy / Part Man, Part Monkey / Goin' / Cali / Back In Your Arms / Brothers Under The Bridge

SPRINGSTEEN: *"It's the alternate route to the road that I took on the records that I released. It tells a similar story but you are going down a different road where all the roadside markers are a little different and the signs are different." (1999)*

It was long rumoured that Springsteen, being a prolific songwriter, had hundreds of songs in the can. Here, at last, was every fan's dream: a four-CD box set of unreleased material spanning his entire career. Making the set meant listening to about 250 songs, whittling them down to 100 and then 80 and deciding to remix from the masters rather than use old stereo mixes. The sound is excellent and there are interesting liner-notes. It does show one of the reasons behind the prolific songwriting, namely that at times Springsteen writes essentially the same song several times until he gets a good version of it. The less committed should go for the cut-down version.

18 TRACKS (1999)

Growin' Up / Seaside Bar Song / Rendezvous / Hearts Of Stone / Where The Bands Are / Loose Ends / I Wanna Be With You / My Love Will Not Let You Down / Lion's Den / Pink Cadillac / Janey Don't You Lose Heart / Sad Eyes / Part Man, Part Monkey / Trouble River / Brothers Under The Bridge / The Fever / The Promise

This single CD selected 15 tracks from the box-set but added three previously unreleased tracks: 'The Fever', 'The Promise', and 'Trouble River'. It features the acoustic version of 'Born In The USA' recorded in 1982. The stand-out tracks include 'Rendezvous', 'The Promise', and 'Sad Eyes'.

LIVE IN NEW YORK CITY (2001)

My Love Will Not Let You Down / Prove It All Night / Two Hearts / Atlantic City / Manision On The Hill / The River / Youngstown / Murder Incorporated / Badlands / Out In The Street / Tenth Avenue Freeze-Out / Land Of Hope And Dreams / American Skin (41 Shots) / Lost In The Flood / Born In The USA / Don't Look Back / Jungleland / Ramrod / If I Should Fall Behind

SPRINGSTEEN: *"The band has always given me the confidence to tackle large themes. Something about the size and sound of the music we make, the depth of the relationships, brings this out in my writing. They give me courage ... During rehearsals the image of the band as this big train coming down the track, rolling into your town, smokestacks blowin', kept recurring to me. In my notebook I had an unfinished song, 'Land of Hope and Dreams' ..."*

Having reconvened the E Street Band (complete with Nils Lofgren and Patti Scialfa) Springsteen returned to touring, demonstrating that the celebrative and communal aspect of his music was stronger than ever. This set was taken from the many nights played at Madison Square Gardens. All the material is strong, and some of the older songs like 'Prove It All Night' and 'Out In The Street' have a depth they didn't have first time round. The CD includes two new songs of considerable stature in 'Land of Hope and Dreams' and 'American Skin (41 Shots)', songs written on the tour that Bruce said had helped him find his rock voice again.

THE RISING (2002)

Lonesome Day / Into The Fire / Waitin' On A Sunny Day / Nothing Man / Countin' On A Miracle / Empty Sky / Worlds Apart / Let's Be Friends (Skin To Skin) / Further On (Up The Road) / The Fuse / Mary's Place / You're Missing / The Rising / Paradise / My City Of Ruins

SPRINGSTEEN: *"Our band was built well over many years, for difficult times. When people wanted a dialogue, a conversation of events, internal and external, we developed a language that suited those moments, a language I hoped would entertain, inspire, comfort, and reveal …* **The Rising** *was a renewal of that conversation and the ideas that forged our band."*

Springsteen's response to 9/11 called forth a remarkable album for this stage in his career. Though many of the songs address the catastrophe in New York they do so often indirectly and all the more powerfully for it. 'My City Of Ruins' was actually written years before and was about Asbury Park. The old fire of the E Street Band is felt but at the same time the record updates the sound without leaving you in any doubt who you're listening to. Brendan O'Brien, a top-flight rock producer, brought fresh ideas not only to the recording process but also to song structure, chords and arrangements. Thus, a track like 'Worlds Apart' surprises with its Eastern-sounding intro, courtesy of the Pakistani singer Asif Ali Khan. A gospel influence is felt on songs like 'Lonesome Day' and 'My City Of Ruins', and 'Let's Be Friends' has a gentleness rarely heard in Springsteen's band music, and puts one in mind of Smokey Robinson and the Miracles.

THE ESSENTIAL BRUCE SPRINGSTEEN (2003)

Blinded By The Light / For You / Spirit In The Night / 4th Of July, Asbury Park (Sandy) / Rosalita (Come Out Tonight) / Thunder Road / Born To Run / Jungleland / Badlands / Darkness On The Edge Of Town / The Promised Land / The River / Hungry Heart / Nebraska / Atlantic City / Born In The USA / Glory Days / Dancing In The Dark / Tunnel Of Love / Brilliant Disguise / Human Touch / Living Proof / Lucky Town / Streets Of Philadelphia / The Ghost Of Tom Joad / The Rising / Mary's Place / Lonesome Day / American Skin (41 Shots) / Land Of Hope And Dreams / From Small Things (Big Things One Day Come) / The Big Payback / Held Up Without A Gun / Trapped / None But The Brave / Missing / Lift Me Up / Viva Las Vegas / County Fair / Code Of Silence / Dead Man Walkin' / Countin' On A Miracle

SPRINGSTEEN: *"We made a lot of music. There are albums and albums worth of stuff sitting in the can." (1995)*

"He's so good, you really want to hit him now and again. He'd come to rehearsal and he'd write five songs in a day, and he'd do that all the time, whenever he felt like it." So said Steve Van Zandt in

1987 looking back on The E Street Band's early years. As if to prove this, a mere four years after *Tracks* had unloaded more than 65 previously-unreleased songs, Springsteen managed to find another 12 to make up a third, bonus CD for this collection in the 'Essential' series, where artists and and bands provide a career overview. It's a better compilation than the *Greatest Hits* and it is interesting to see five tracks appear from the first two albums. Perhaps Springsteen himself had re-assessed his early music, prompted by the two albums' steadily rising critical reputation.

VIDEO AND DVD

Springsteen's concert performances are currently available on DVD as *The Complete Video Anthology 1978-2000* (2001), *Blood Brothers* (2001), *Live In New York City* (2001), and *Live In Barcelona* (2003).

SONGWRITING THEORY
A BEGINNER'S GUIDE

This is a quick guide to songwriting theory to explain symbols such as the Roman numeral chord system used in the main part of the book. To explore the background theory and practice of songwriting in more detail, see my other Backbeat books, in particular *How To Write Songs On Guitar* (2000), *The Songwriting Sourcebook* (2003), and *Melody* (2004).

The major scale

The chords that a song uses, its melody and its sense of key are derived from the major scale. There are other types of scale, but none is as important to songwriting for providing the chords over which you sing. The major scale is a sequence of eight notes ascending in steps to cover an octave: the distance from one note to the next note with the same name. The steps in the scale are determined by this pattern of intervals: tone, tone, semitone, tone, tone, tone, semitone. Pick any note on any guitar string below the 5th fret and then play up the string, using these fret distances: 2 2 1 2 2 2 1. That creates a major scale from the note on which you started. On the piano find the note C and simply play up the white keys until you arrive at C an octave higher. That's the same pattern.

The roman numeral system

Putting aside the eighth note (which has the same letter name as the first) the major scale has seven different notes. The chords built on these are numbered in roman numerals: I, II, III, IV, V, VI and VII. You don't need to know how chords are formed to write songs. These seven chords sound good together and generate the sense of a key.

These roman numerals signify possible tonal 'roles' that a chord of a given pitch and type can play. This means that a single chord like C major can play the 'role' of I, IV or V depending on whether the key is C major, G major or F major.

Here are the chords of A major, whose scale is A B C# D E F# G#:

I	II	III	IV	V	VI	VII
A	Bm	C#m	D	E	F#m	G#dim

Notice that chords I, IV and V are major; chords II, III and VI are minor; and chord VII is diminished. As a result, VII is hardly ever used and is normally replaced with a bVII (major) chord, which here would be a G chord (see the mixolydian song in Section 2).

The beauty of the roman numeral system is that chord sequences can be written independently of pitch. I can talk about a I-VI-IV-V progression without specifying the key. This can be useful if at a later date I want to change the key because the original one didn't suit my voice. You can write out the progressions of whole songs as roman numerals only and then just write the desired key at the top. With practice you get to know which chords fit the numerals in the popular guitar keys.

The minor scale

Minor keys are more complicated than major keys. There is only one major scale pattern, but there are several variations on the minor scale. Each variation results in alternative chord options. The scales themselves we do not need to delve into. Instead, we can go straight to a list of songwriting chords for the minor key. As with major and minor chords, so every major key has a *relative minor* which shares almost all the same chords. Compare the chords for C major with that of its relative minor, A minor:

I	II	III	IV	V	VI	VII
C	Dm	Em	F	G	Am	Bdim

I	II	III	IV	V	VI	VII
Am	Bdim	C	Dm	Em	F	G

We have the same set of chords, they are merely in a different order. More precisely, they have changed their harmonic functions. Harmonic function and pitch identity are different things. The chord G in the key of C major has the same pitch identity as the G in the key of A minor – they are the same chord. But when G is chord V in C major it has a different harmonic function to being chord VII in A minor.

For convenience, we can describe this version of A minor as 'modal' A minor (the notes A B C D E F G) or to be precise the Aeolian mode on A. There is a group of seven scales called modes that historically pre-dates the modern system of keys. One of them became the major scale. Another, the Aeolian mode, is also known as the 'natural minor' scale.

Another consequence of A minor and C major sharing the same chords is that we still have that problematic diminished chord on B. Instead of being chord VII it is now chord II – which in some ways is more awkward. So, as with VII in the major key, the diminished chord II of the minor key tends to be replaced by a first inversion of chord VII – in A natural minor, G/B – or a second inversion of chord V – Em/B. Thus we arrive at the composite minor key chords first described in Section 2.

A songwriter's composite minor key

I	III	IV	(IV^)	V	(Vm)	VI	VII
Am	C	Dm	(D)	E	(Em)	F	G

This gives you eight chords to choose from for a minor key song. Remember that all eight minor-key chords are capable of first and second inversions (8 x 3 = 24).

SONG INDEX

49129

ACKNOWLEDGEMENTS

Quotations are taken from the following publications: Bruce Springsteen's lyric book *Songs* (1998, revised 2003), *Bruce Springsteen In His Own Words* compiled by John Duffy (Omnibus 1993), *Bruce Springsteen: The Rolling Stone Files* (Sidgwick and Jackson, 1997), *Springsteen: Blinded By The Light* by Patrick Humphries and Chris Hunt (Plexus 1985), back issues of *Guitarist*, *Mojo*, *Q*, *Uncut*, *Guitar World*, and the website www.greasylake.org. For their involvement in the preparation of this book I would like to thank Nigel Osborne, Tony Bacon, Phil Richardson, Mark Brend, John Morrish, Paul Cooper and Kim Devlin.

ABOUT THE AUTHOR

Rikky Rooksby is a guitar teacher, songwriter/composer, and writer on popular music. He is the author of the Backbeat titles *How To Write Songs On Guitar* (2000), *Inside Classic Rock Tracks* (2001), *Riffs* (2002), *The Songwriting Sourcebook* (2003), *Chord Master* (2004) and *Melody* (2004). He contributed to *Classic Guitars Of The Fifties*, *The Guitar: the complete guide for the player*, and *Roadhouse Blues* (2003). He has also written *The Guitarist's Guide to the Capo* (Artemis 2003), *The Complete Guide To The Music Of Fleetwood Mac* (revised ed. 2004), *The Complete Guide To The Music Of Madonna* (revised ed. 2004), 14 Fastforward guitar tutor books, four in the *First Guitar* series; transcribed and arranged over forty chord songbooks of music including Bob Dylan, Bob Marley, the Stone Roses, David Bowie, Eric Clapton, Travis, The Darkness, and *The Complete Beatles*; and co-authored *100 Years 100 Songs*. He has written articles on rock musicians for the new *Dictionary Of National Biography* (OUP), and published interviews, reviews, articles and transcriptions in magazines such as *Guitar Techniques*, *Total Guitar*, *Guitarist*, *Bassist*, *Bass Guitar Magazine*, *The Band*, *Record Collector*, *Sound On Sound*, and *Making Music*, where he wrote the monthly 'Private Pluck' guitar column. He is a member of the Guild of International Songwriters and Composers, the Sibelius Society, and the Vaughan Williams Society. Visit his website at www.rikkyrooksby.com